From Farm Boy to Fighter Pilot and Beyond

Set Goals
Achieve Them
Finish Strong

Harold E. (Hal) Watson
Colonel, USAF Ret.

From Farm Boy to Fighter Pilot and Beyond
Copyright © 2019 by Harold E. Watson

Published in the United States of America

ISBN: 9781793176370

Cover by Suzanne Parada, www.paradadesign.com

Dedication

Clearly, the most intelligent thing I have ever done is to ask Bette Jayne Douglas to marry me. Now, more than half a century later she has been my best friend, my help mate, mother to our children, and World Class Wife. I cannot give her enough praise, nor can I imagine my life without her.

We have been blessed with two boys who wisely married great women. Together they have added four grandchildren, the oldest engaged to add a fine young man to our family.

For many years the family has been asking me to write an autobiography. While B.J. and our sons have lived most of my nearly eight decades, they only know a few snippets of the first two. Of course, the grandchildren only know a little of our legacy.

It is for B.J. and the family, some yet to be born, that this book is dedicated.

Acknowledgements

In addition, I want to recognize the formative role that my parents played. They instilled a strong work ethic, a moral code, and positive attitude to pursue demanding goals.

Brother Bill, his wife Glenda, and their two girls, Susan and Sallie, are instrumental in continuing the Watson legacy in Indiana. They were the strong support to our parents. In addition, they provided several of the pictures and stories in the book. I am eternally grateful to them.

Alexandra Ward took my initial interest in writing a memoir and taught me how to take various themes and meld them into an autobiography. Without her instruction, editing, and encouragement, the book may not have happened. Thank you for persevering and your kind review of the manuscript.

Similarly, David Laschinger and Ken Arthur, accomplished writers and friends, provided technical expertise and encouragement to finish the project.

Thanks to Dr. Ken Reed and General Bob Dempsey for reviewing the manuscript, making suggestions and generously providing comments.

Finally, thanks to Suzanne Parada for the creative design of the cover.

Table of Contents

Introduction

Tombstones often have the date of birth, date of death, and a hyphen between the dates. This autobiography addresses the hyphen, what happened along the way between my birth and yet to occur death. It also addresses the importance of setting goals, achieving them and finishing strong.

I did a lot of thinking, talking, and ruminating as I began to consider how I would recall and organize the nearly eight decades. In one of those moments, the title came to me. "**From Farm Boy to Fighter Pilot and Beyond**" really encapsulates my life.

I was raised in a very small community as a **Farm Boy**, set a goal and became a **Fighter Pilot** for 26 years, and my retired life after the Air Force has been **Beyond** what I could ask or think.

My **Farm Boy** life really began in a little farming community. Our family was loving and nurturing, and I enjoyed farming and working in our store. However, I soon became convinced that I had been imbued at conception with a desire and ability to be a pilot. Dad found a newspaper article about the approval to start a USAF Academy and I set a goal to graduate from there.

It took three applications and a couple of years of civilian college to qualify for entrance into the Air Force Academy. The third application was accepted and my desire to be a fighter pilot was about to get started. Graduation from The Academy four years later was a major milestone and a goal accomplished.

While at The Academy, I had the blessing of meeting Bette Jayne Douglas (B.J.). We were married the day after graduation. More than a half century has passed since those beginnings. It hasn't always been a floral lined highway; there have been many chuck holes along our road. But our commitment to each other and to Jesus Christ as our Savior and Lord, made the trip exciting, fruitful and fulfilling.

The **Fighter Pilot** phase began with being a Distinguished Graduate from pilot training and earning the assignment to fly the

RF-4C Phantom II. Our Air Force career involved 26 years, 15 permanent assignments throughout the United States and in four foreign countries and moving every couple of years. I flew 202 combat missions in Vietnam. My final command assignments were as tactical wing commander and air division commander in Panama.

The Air Force period brought us two sons, Derek and Doug. They expanded our family by marrying Kelly and Christy and adding four grandchildren. More about their families in later chapters.

With the Air Force career ended, the next phase of our lives began with a formal retirement ceremony at Bergstrom AFB, Texas. I officially retired as a Colonel from the USAF on July 1, 1990.

The **And Beyond** phase of life began on July 5, 1990 when I entered the corporate world as a contractor for DynCorp Aviation Services. After five years at DynCorp, I moved to several other companies culminating in starting BJAerospace LLC. We continue to operate BJAerospace to provide aircraft sales and acquisition, pilot services, and other aviation related support.

B.J. and I are from humble beginnings by the world's measurement. However, we are from loving parents who strived that we would expand their worlds. We want to pass the legacy that it isn't where you start, it is important where you finish. The Watson Legacy of hard work, integrity, accountability, and education started by our parents has led us down paths that they, or even we, could not have imagined.

B.J.'s support and tolerance for a rather nomadic life not only made it all possible; she made it fulfilling, interesting, and at a much higher level from where we had started. A general who would later become the Chief of Staff of the Air Force wrote her a letter calling her a "world-class wife of a wing commander." I call her the "*Wind Beneath My Wings*" and my wingman for life.

I hope that you will read "*From Farm Boy to Fighter Pilot and Beyond*" with joy. I pray you will find heart-lifting stories that will encourage you to think about the hyphen between your birth and death and you will commit to finishing strong.

Chapter 1: Born in the Big City but Headed to the Farm

Life Began in Hammond, Indiana (1940-1945)

Born as World War II was beginning in Europe and before Pearl Harbor, I was too late to be of the "Greatest Generation" and too early to be a "Baby Boomer". Yet, I was right on time to be raised in the age of the 50s. The TV show, *Happy Days,* and the movie, *Hoosiers*, would later chronicle the lifestyles of my generation and growing up in rural Indiana.

I was blessed to be a child of Ralph and Mildred Watson who survived The Great Depression. Dad was second of six children born to William and Maude Watson on the farm in Indiana. Even though the family was linked to the farm, education was essential to them. All six were able to attend college. The two youngest ones graduated with PhDs with the help of the GI Bill earned from their WWII service in the Army and Navy. Unfortunately, the only girl died soon after graduating from college from tuberculosis, a disease common for that time.

Dad and his siblings grew up on a farm just north of the small town of Graysville, Indiana. They farmed corn, soy beans, and wheat and raised and milked dairy cows. They were also involved in sports, including refereeing basketball and other sports to make a little extra money during the Great Depression. However, the small farm was insufficient to sustain the entire family. Dad and his oldest brother went to college at Elon College in North Carolina. After completing a year, they could no longer afford the tuition and returned to Indiana. Without work there, they began working on a migrant farm team beginning with harvesting strawberries in the South and working the wheat harvest as it ripened going north into Manitoba. Dad would often tell stories of cutting wheat and feeding it into the steam engine driven thrashing machines and their travels through the various parts of the U.S. and Canada.

Dad is on top, his brother Ural on the right,

While working at a strawberry farm in Arkansas, Dad met Mildred Taylor. She was the daughter of Arthur and Suzy Taylor and had three siblings. After a long-distance courtship, they married and moved back to Indiana where dad picked up jobs in the local community. Hearing of the big money in the factories in Northern Indiana, he packed up with his new bride and moved to Hammond. With Dad working in the factories and Mom working in a drug store, they added me to make a family of three. Less than a year later, the attack on Pearl Harbor would force the United States into war in the Pacific quickly followed by war in Europe. Dad received a deferment from World War II due to his critical job manufacturing war machines and my entry into the world.

Almost coincident with the end of the war, the second son was born on August 29, 1945. He was named after our paternal grandfather, William, and maternal grandfather, Arthur. William Arthur (Bill) completed our family.

Now with two boys and the war over, Dad began reflecting on how to best raise the boys. He quickly decided that the urban life of

Hammond was not the place. He always wanted to move back to the farm community where he was born and raised. He and Mom were prudent with their money and had been saving for that possibility. During their time in Hammond, his dad had called to tell him that a large wooded area that Dad knew very well was going to be sold and asked Dad if he would like to buy it. Dad quickly said yes. In those days, a yes was as good as a contract. The paper work would be finalized when he made the next trip home.

I have only a few memories of Hammond, starting kindergarten, brother Bill entering the family, Dad firing his shotgun into the air to celebrate the end of WWII and our dog, Bomber. Interestingly, Dad bought the shot gun before America entered the war. Living in Hammond, he was able to hunt pheasant in Northern Indiana and quail when he visited the family back home. Nearly 80 years later, I still have that shotgun and it has been used in hunting from Indiana to Idaho by our boys and me. Today, it is in an honored place. To protect the legacy, it is regularly cleaned and available. Perhaps the time will come to take it to the skeet range and relive some of the hunting trips with Dad and Bill while teaching our grandsons those skills.

The boys and I did use that gun and the first one that Dad had given me to go rabbit hunting on a winter trip to Indiana many years later. My mom was true to her farm wife talents and fixed rabbit gravy for dinner. As was the rule when I was hunting as a teenager, the boys had to eat what they killed. They cautiously ate, but B.J. respectfully declined.

Now with the woods purchased and the war over, Dad and Mom made plans to move back to Graysville, Indiana, a population of about 100 people, one intersection, three general stores, two gas stations, a barber shop with post office in the back, and a Methodist Church. In retrospect, I don't think Mom was excited to leave the city life to go back to the farm. She enjoyed the modern conveniences and friends that they had made there.

This picture was taken in the early 1960s,
but the town hasn't changed much since 1946.
Our new store is the white building on the left.
The small building on the right was the barber shop and post office.
The original Watson's General was to the left of the stop sign.

They purchased a home and one of the country stores. However, the income wasn't quite enough to support a family, so dad took a job in a factory about 30 miles away. His experience in the large factory in Hammond served him well and he quickly became a foreman.

Transitioning to Life in Graysville, Indiana (1945-1958).

Mom, Dad, Bill, our dog Bomber, and I moved into the newly purchased house in 1945. The house was a typical early century two story model with a big front porch ringed with columns and gingerbread trim. The lot was an acre with very large front yard that would become the favorite play area for the neighborhood kids. The downstairs rooms consisted of a living room, master bedroom, kitchen and utility room. Upstairs were two bedrooms and a large landing with a big round window. The upstairs was just right for Bill and me.

Our "New Home" in Graysville 1946

However, there were none of the luxuries that Mom had enjoyed in the city house in Hammond. There was no air conditioning, unless you considered wind through the cracks under the doors and around the windows. There was no indoor plumbing. For water, we had a shallow well with manual pump. There was a bucket to carry water from the well to the kitchen and a big dipper to transfer it for drinking or cooking. One tradition was that if you got the last of the water from the bucket, you had to refill it. Bill and I became very proficient at quietly manipulating the dipper to not hit it against the porcelain lined bucket that made the empty signal. The slightest sound resulted in the admonition to go to the outdoor pump and fill it up.

The indoor bathroom in the Hammond house became a wishful memory and was replaced in this home by an outhouse about 75 feet from the back door. We never quite understood why the broad seat had two holes of adult height and a lower level hole for a child. Did the builder of the outhouse anticipate the entire family going at the same time? Walking barefoot to the outhouse at night was not advised due to Dad's indiscriminate tossing of chewing tobacco plugs from the back door. And we could only imagine what might be lurking in the dark recesses of the outhouse. Smells were controlled by judiciously sprinkling lime on what you had left in the dark expanse below. Since we owned the general store, toilet paper was always available thus avoiding the time-held traditions of Sears-Roebuck Catalog pages.

Heat for the main house was supplied by coal stoves, one in the living room and one in the kitchen. We had electricity that initially was only for lighting. Mom cooked and baked in that coal range until additional electrical capacity and wiring was installed. It was a happy day when Mom left the coal fired stove for a new electric stove and oven.

I had an early introduction to "chores." In addition to the water that had to be carried from the well to the house, coal was brought in from the coal house and ashes were carried out. A basketball goal was mounted on the side of the coal house. Ashes from the stove were carefully spread beside the coal house to make a basketball court. The rain and footprints of aspiring Hoosier kids pounded the ashes into a firm foundation for dribbling, cut, and shoot. I learned about atmospheric laws by playing basketball outside in Indiana winters. As the ball cooled, the gas pressure would decrease, and the ball couldn't be dribbled. I would take the ball inside, sit it on top of the stove until the heat brought up the pressure. (Maybe Tom Brady knows about this principle as well.) This early lesson in physics would be repeated when learning about airplanes and how they fly.

This picture was taken as the Old Store was being torn down.

Watson's General Store was the result of the purchase of the business of one of three general stores in Graysville. It had been a fixture of the community, even in Dad's early years. It was a large brick structure located at the only intersection in town. Unfortunately, Dad was unable to purchase the building and had to lease it from the former owners. The East/West State Highway 154 ran from Sullivan (our county seat to the east) to Illinois to the west. The North/South State Highway 63 ran from Merom (the closest town south) to Terre Haute (our largest town 25 miles to the north).

The store was the epitome of a family enterprise. Dad's uncle, Ray Watson, was the lead clerk and was there most of the time. Mom took over when Uncle Ray needed a break and Dad would often work there when he returned from the factory in Terre Haute. I was quickly integrated into the operation.

Watson's General Store was well stocked

The economy of Watson's General Store was based on staples such as canned goods, meat, vegetables, etc. We also carried seed corn, some yard goods and sewing supplies, and other necessities of life for our customers. We bought eggs from the farmers and sold them to our customers for a small profit. In those days, organic (range free) eggs were the norm. My job was to check them to ensure there were no embryos to surprise an early morning breakfast cook. I built a contraption to speed the process by cutting a hole the size of the egg in the bottom of a can. I then added a light bulb and wire to focus the light up through the hole. Holding the egg over the hole, I could see if there were embryos inside the egg. We stocked hardware that small things could be built, and quick repairs made on farm tractors and other equipment. We also had a large candy selection of both bars and bulk candies. In those days, it seemed that everyone used some form of tobacco. We carried various brands of cigarettes and pipe and chewing tobacco. As we now know, tobacco caused early death for many. In many ways, the retail section of Cracker Barrel has copied the concept of the old General Store, except for the tobacco.

During the planting season, we sold seed corn and soy beans in large bushel bags for the local famers and stocked a varied assortment of garden vegetable and flower seeds. At harvest we bought sweet corn, tomatoes and watermelons from local farmers and gardeners and sold them in the store.

Our first gas pumps were of the hand pump variety. Gas was stored below ground. To dispense it into cars, there was a long-handled hand pump that brought the gas into a 10-gallon glass reservoir on top of the pump. Gas levels were etched into the glass. The customer ordered the number of gallons they wanted, and we hand pumped it into the reservoir with gravity delivering it into the car, truck or tractor. If the customer wanted more than 10 gallons, we refilled the reservoir as often as needed. The price of the sale was calculated by multiplying the cost per gallons times the gallons delivered. Another opportunity to use my math lessons. We were excited when the gas company provided the electric pumps that calculated both gallons and cost.

This picture was taken at a museum in Weatherford, TX but is an exact replica of the gas pumps at Watson's General Store.

In the center of the store was a very tall, rotund coal stove. It was about seven feet tall and three feet in diameter. It would probably hold an entire bucket of coal. There were benches all around the stove. It became the local spot to loaf, catch up on community news, or just gossip. ("Loaf" was the term then for "Hanging Out" now.) After years of providing heat for the entire store, it developed a rather large crack. No problem, we went down the street to Ross Ransford's blacksmith shop and manufactured a rod that was girdled around the stove's circumference with a connector that permitted tightening this contraption to return the integrity of the stove. It survived several more years with this simple fix.

Dad's parents, William and Maude Watson, had operated a farm and dairy business north of town before the Great Depression. Grandpa Will was involved in local politics and had been a Township Trustee. Consequently, the Watson family was rather well known throughout the local area and Sullivan County. When Grandpa and Grandma became "Empty Nesters" they moved to a small house on about 40 acres located a mile east of Graysville. My earliest memories of them was Grandma in her apron fixing family meals. They had a few milk cows and chickens. I was always interested in how they used a hand-cranked separator to divide the milk and cream and used some of the cream to churn butter. Organic food was a Watson staple before it became cool and a marketing slogan.

Grandpa Will and Grandma Maude Watson

Grandpa died while helping Dad move some livestock. They were driving in Dad's pickup when Grandpa had a heart attack, took a deep breath and leaned across the seat onto Dad's shoulder, and quietly passed away. He had just turned 65. His funeral was well attended and the procession to the cemetery was several miles long.   I didn't know him well. At the end of the funeral Mom and Dad led Bill and me to his open casket to say goodbye.

From Left, Dad and me, Aunt Josephine, Mom, Uncle Gene, Aunt Betty, Grandma Maude and Grandpa Will

Grandma Maude continued to live in that house for a brief time, then moved into the master bedroom on our first floor. We farmed the "Home Place" and she rented out the house for several more years. After a few years in our house, a nice trailer home was purchased and installed on our lot. Grandma lived there several years enjoying family visits and neighbors. I did get to know her but have regretted not spending more time with her when she was living with us.

Chapter 2: Life on the Farm

This Old House

As mentioned earlier, the original house was a classic farm house. However, in this situation, classic meant old, no central air or heat, no plumbing, and issues brought on by age and termites.

Several upgrades were made over a period of a dozen years. With the help of a few people, Dad hand-dug a septic tank and the interconnecting tiles to handle the waste water and sewage. Indoor plumbing was installed in the utility room. A new water well was drilled to provide the water needed for the new plumbing. The old coal cooking range was replaced with an electric stove and oven and the electrical wiring was upgraded.

When Grandma Maude moved in with us, the downstairs master bedroom was converted to her sitting room and the small adjacent room her bedroom. A kerosene stove was added to give her heat. Mom and Dad moved upstairs into Bill's bedroom and Bill moved his bed into my room. Since there was no heat up there, a hole was cut in the floor of each of the bedrooms and adjustable registers were installed to permit heat from the rooms below to rise upstairs. Obviously, this was inadequate by modern standards. In the winter, we learned to quickly undress and jump into bed. Bill and I would often select our clothes for the next day and neatly put them under the covers with us so that we could dress in semi-warm clothes rather than the near-freezing ones in the closet and dresser. Once dressed, we would quickly run downstairs to the kitchen where the coal stove was much warmer, and breakfast was ready.

Summer in Indiana could be a hot, humid challenge. We opened the windows in each bedroom giving a North-South flow of air. A large fan was installed in the window of the bedroom shared by Bill and me. It seemed to only recirculate hot, humid air. Somehow, we all survived through both summer and winter.

The "classic" house had many shortcomings. On an afternoon, Mom went to the door to find two women who had driven by and were enchanted with the house. They asked if she had any antiques. She answered, "No, just this old house." They answered, "Don't you just love it?" She replied, "No." The conversation was over. This house could not have been efficiently or effectively modernized in an age well before HGTV and "*Fixer Upper*." At Mom's insistence, plans were made to replace this classic with a modern single-story home, the architecture now known as "Mid-Century Modern." However, the new house would have to wait for many years.

Saturday Night Lights in Graysville

Graysville was the small-town center for the farming community within a four or five-mile radius. Saturday was the evening when the farm families came to town to shop and exchange news of the previous week. Consequently, Watson's General Store became a gathering spot for our loyal customers. The customers of the two other stores tended to go to their favorite store, but there also was an intermixing of the various loyalties to ensure that the customer got the best deal in town.

The earlier mentioned round stove was the center of conversation. Men tended to gather on the front porch or on benches on one side of the stove while the women congregated on the other side. Perhaps too much togetherness during the week led to a desire for the men and women to separate and share with others the events of that week. Besides, the guys wanted to talk about tractors, farming and hunting while the women were more interested in families or a newly discovered recipe.

Much of the conversations had to do with farming business, the price of crops now and what the bid was for future crops. Interest rates were critical because most farmers borrowed money to plant the crops in the Spring and would repay the loans in the Fall. The thin profit margins could be eaten if the interest rate was high.

The highlight of the evening was the "Drawing." Tickets were earned with purchases from the store. One ticket was awarded for each twenty-five cents in products purchased. Tickets were deposited in a large lard can with the stubs being held by the customer. At 8:00pm, Dad would select one of the younger kids to do the drawing for the prizes to be awarded that night. First Prize was always $3.00, Second Prize was a pair of lady's nylons that could be exchanged for the right color and size, Third Prize was a canned vegetable or fruit and the Final Prize was a six-pack of soda pop, usually Cokes.

For the children, there was the opportunity to play outdoor games that included the stalwarts of Tag, Hide-And-Seek and Kick-The-Can. Since our store and house were less than 50 yards apart, the kids tended to start on the front porch of the store and move to our front yard. This arrangement allowed the kids to have a wonderful time running off energy while the parents shopped, loafed, and visited in the store without worrying about what evil might lurk in the darkness. We kids played through the evening until the parents decided it was time to leave. These games allowed us to forge friendships that are well remembered today. Regulars at the Saturday Night games were Bill, Jay Mike, Jane, Suzie, Jerry, Londa, Terry and many others. We could have been the basis for *"The Little Rascals"* TV Show. Thanks to Jerry, we still are connected through a Facebook Group, entitled "If you ever lived in Graysville."

When the drawing was over at our store, some customers moved a couple of blocks up the street to another store that held their "Drawing" at 9:00. Sometimes, people would hang out there after the drawing to watch television, one of only a few in town. I remember that some of us went there to watch "Saturday Night Fights."

Looking through the lens of the 21st Century, all of this seems very boring, unimaginative and unsophisticated. On the contrary, in rural America of the 1940's and 1950's, it was not any of those things. Rather, it was the epitome of community and sharing. Deep philosophical discussions of politics and economics were routinely addressed. I learned my first lessons of respect for others, freedom, capitalism, return on investment of demanding work, and kindness while listening in on discourses around the circular stove and similar gathering places. Those lessons have served me well in today's environment of "Me First," hateful speech, lack of respect, and laziness. It is a great tragedy that these basic lessons have been lost in Washington, DC and Wall Street. It is even worse that the life style and people have been termed "Deplorable" by a few national leaders.

Saturday night was also pay time for Bill and me. We received an "allowance" for certain chores around the house and store. Our base allowance was a quarter and we held it closely. As we grew in age and responsibilities, our Saturday Pay Out was increased to a dollar or more. As Dad paid us, he would always say, "Now boys, don't spend all of that in one place, and don't get off of the porch." Of course, the porch was connected to the store and following that admonition, we would have returned it back to the store's income. While he was mostly kidding, it did make the point that we should be prudent even with a few quarters.

The store also taught entrepreneurship. I learned early in life that hard work and prior planning paid off. We bought merchandise from Hulman Wholesale, gas from Phillips 66, eggs from local farmers and we determined honest prices to sell them that would yield a profit to feed our family and build a business. Saturday night after the store was closed, we would go home to the living room, put the money in the middle of the floor and account for our purchases and sales to determine if we had, in fact, made a profit for the week. Money was deposited into both checking and savings accounts yielding another "life-lesson" for Bill and me.

About the time I became a young teenager, yet too young to drive, there was a bus line that ran from Terre Haute through Graysville, stopping at our store, to Sullivan, the county seat about 8 miles east. We could get on the bus, ride to Sullivan, go to the movie, buy some popcorn and soda, and return home on the bus in a few hours for only a dollar or two. Obviously, our few guys riding once a week didn't make for a profitable bus line and it was shut down after about a year.

Of course, we always looked up to the older boys who had cars and motorcycles. Lester lived across the street and got a Model T. I thought it was great to ride in the rumble seat.   A more adventurous boy lived about a mile out of town. His nickname, even used by his parents, was Ding Bat. Ding Bat had a very cool Indian Motorcycle. My parents made very strong threats about what would happen if they caught me riding it. I believed them and always avoided the temptation to go for a ride. Later Shan bought the first Corvette Convertible in the county. I did persuade him for a ride. That ride has resulted in me owning two Corvette Convertibles in the past several years. He traded it for a 1957 Thunderbird. I am sure Shan wishes he had kept both of those early model sports cars.

Party Line Telephones

The local telephone system was especially interesting when viewed through today's digital glasses. The parents of my best friend, Jay Mike, operated the system, from the switchboard to the telephone instrument. Jay Mike's dad ran the wires throughout the system and repaired the phones. His mom was the head operator of the switch board. Because there were limits on the number of lines that could be run from the "Central" office throughout the township, many homes and business were on "Party Lines". Often there could be four or more homes on the same line. Each home had a distinctive number and ring sequence.

Our home phone number was 7G10. The first number, 7, was the line number. G10 meant that our ring sequence was a long ring and three short rings. Our store number was 7G12. Again, 7 was the line and G12 was two short rings. Consequently, since both phones were on line 7, we could easily tell if the call was for home or the store. Moreover, if the store was closed or no one at home, we could answer the phone in the other place.

This is the phone that hung on the wall in our first house. The store had a desk model.

A page from the Telephone Book. Both our House and Store are listed on the bottom right side

Interesting things occurred because of more than one home being on the same line. Certain people were obsessed with other people's business. Consequently, If the nosey person wanted to know why someone was calling their neighbor, they would wait until their neighbor answered the phone, then quietly pick up their receiver to listen to the latest news, gossip, happenings, etc. It was widely held that one older widow tied her receiver to her favorite rocker so that when she wanted to listen to someone else's call, she didn't have to get up from the rocker.

Jay Mike's mom as the head operator at the Central Switchboard, much like Earnestine on Laugh-In TV. (Go to You Tube, Nxp5Y8UT70Q.) for a short introduction to small town switchboard operators.) Her switchboard was on the second story of a house just south of the road intersection in the heart of Graysville. With windows facing both north and south along the main highway, she could observe most of the activities in the town. If I wanted to call my dad from a friend's phone, I could pick up their receiver, if no one was on the line, I would crank the phone once and "Central" would answer. I never gave a number, I just said, "I would like to speak to Dad please" and she would recognize my voice and call our home.

One Thanksgiving, Dad's oldest brother, a vice president of an East Coast firm, was visiting us. His president needed to talk with him and placed a person-to-person call to Ural Watson at Graysville, Indiana, 7G10. However, we had gone to another brother's house for dinner. When we didn't answer, the operator told them that she had seen us leave to go to Uncle Gay's house and asked if they would like her to call there. Of course, they said yes, and the call was quickly re-routed and completed. As anyone could imagine, the sophisticated East Coast corporate leadership had great fun commenting about the call and the one-horse-town operator who knew everyone's business. In today's connected world, we have an app to track our friends and family. However, the app also has caused us to lose the personal connection enjoyed years ago.

Expanding Watson Holdings

Dad and Mom, products of the Great Depression, were determined to live better and leave a legacy for their children and grandchildren. They started with the store and the woods and Dad took a job in Terre Haute while Mom periodically worked in the store. They also looked for ways to increase income sources and diversified by buying an apple orchard and adding acreage to the woods.

Bill and I learned to work on the farm at an early age. We raised corn, soybeans and wheat and periodically ran cattle, sheep and pigs. Watermelons and cantaloupe thrived in the sandy ground of our farm.

Bill and I and a crop of cantaloupe on our farm

The apple orchard was interesting for a time, but quickly became a challenge. While it seemed rather easy to buy some trees already bearing fruit, it soon became back-breakingly obvious that orchards demand work. The trees must be fertilized, trimmed and sprayed. Unfortunately, Dad broke a rib while trimming the trees, or he said it was broken because he would lie on the floor and Bill and I would jump on him. Regardless of the cause, he was in significant pain. But he pressed on with his work responsibilities in the steel mill, farm and store. Then comes harvest and marketing. All must successfully occur before there is income.

Dad, having been raised on a farm that used horses rather than tractors, decided he needed a couple of horses to work the orchard and other areas around the farm. These horses bore no resemblance to the Budweiser Clydesdales. Nope, they were work horses of the common variety.

The horses did a decent job plowing the large garden that Mom planted, and they pulled the wagon in the corn field to glean corn left by the picking machines and pulling the wagon while tending to the orchard. During harvest, I rode in the wagon and drove the horses to gather the corn or baskets of apples we had previously picked and left setting by the trees. I was often confused by "Gee" and "Haw," which was left and which right. Bill often rode with us and became more involved as he grew.

We transferred the baskets of apples from the wagon into the pickup and delivered them to our house where they were sorted. The best apples went to the store to sell to our regular customers, some were run through the cider press and others were wrapped in newspaper and buried to preserve them to sell out of season. When they were dug up later in the year they were just as good as when we had buried them. The fresh cider was bottled and sold in the store. The pressed apples, core and all, were fed to the pigs. Once again, conservation of assets was a lesson to be remembered for a lifetime.

After a few years, the work load of the orchard overtook the small profit margin and it was sold. Soon the horses were sold and replaced by a tractor. The tractor was owned by Dad's brother and became an unfortunate negative with his wife. When that tractor became old and underpowered, we bought a new Ford tractor. Initially, Dad was reticent to borrow money to buy it. Bill and I offered that we had savings that were just setting in the bank and could be used to buy the tractor. He reluctantly agreed and we were happy to have a new tractor. Dad paid us back that Fall with the profit from the crops.

The final addition to the Watson holdings was the purchase of a farm adjacent to the woods. It had been a portion of a much larger Watson Farm. Unfortunately, much of that original farm had been leveraged to buy additional land before the Great Depression. As the Depression intensified and the economy tanked, many acres were lost to creditors. The remaining 116 acres were owned by Dad's uncle. When he was killed in an automobile accident, we rented and farmed the land. Dad later purchased it.

New Store

The State of Indiana decided that State Highway 63 north of the Graysville intersection should be widened and straightened and the intersection improved. Watson's General Store and a portion of our front yard were in the way. Since Dad was only leasing the building, the state wanted the property and couldn't care less what Dad did with the contents. Through strong negotiation he convinced them of his potential losses and that he should receive compensation. They agreed and provided the funds necessary to build a new building on the front of the lot that our home occupied and move the contents of the old store to that new building. Another lesson was learned, you need to negotiate to protect your own interests.

Moving the store wasn't easy. An old barn and the house in which Uncle Ray was living had to be removed and the building built. The summer of my high school junior year became the time of education in construction. The old barn was torn down and Uncle Ray's house was moved. Interestingly, moving the house became a topic of great discussion amongst the neighborhood and various farmers. Is it torn down and scrapped or jacked up and put on a truck? How about putting it on runners and pulling it to another location? A neighbor was a few years older than me and he was confident that his new, high powered tractor could pull it anywhere. The plan was baked -- jack it up, put some skids under it and he would pull it away. Everything went well for a time, and people gathered while he positioned his tractor. In his enthusiasm to prove both himself and his tractor in front of the crowd, he too quickly popped the clutch and the tractor jumped, then died, much to his chagrin and the laughs of the crowd. With the tractor re-started, it did get it going. Fortunately, for him, the laughs turned to cheers and his integrity and his tractor's power were proven. Uncle Ray retired and moved into a small house on the east side of Graysville. Mom became the chief clerk and supervised the transition planning for the new store.

With the barn and house gone, work began on the store building. The slab was poured, and concrete blocks erected to form the shell. A flat roof was added. A neighbor who was recently back from serving in the Air Force came to help. He, Bill, and I provided much of the manual labor to build the store. With the building complete, the shelving, counters, refrigerators, and merchandise were moved from the old to the new store.

A grand opening inaugurated the store. Several of our wholesale providers donated merchandise to be given away on opening day. Some of our customers sent flowers. The building was about one-third the size of the old store. Consequently, the old stove wouldn't fit and was replaced by a new propane furnace and a small lavatory was added. Seed corn and several other items were deleted due to lack of space. But the basics were there.

Grand Opening of Watson's Store
Complete with Balloons and Flowers

With the old buildings gone, the old store gone, and the new store operational, the new road could be built. Construction of the road in front of our house and store required digging the roadbed to about 4 feet below the normal grade. A huge rain made a pond that dried a bit into a big mud hole. Several people tried to drive through the mud but were stuck. No problem, I used my growing entrepreneurial skills to take the tractor and chain and pull them out, gladly accepting any gratuity they wished to bestow.

While the mud was still in place, Mom looked out of the store window to see an elderly friend struggling to get across the road and clutching a bunch of clothes in her hand. Mom and I went out on the porch to learn that she was mowing her lawn and put her hand under the lawn mower while it was running. A portion of her hand and a couple of fingers were severed. Mom called the lady's daughter-in-law, we loaded them both into our station wagon, and I began driving them to the hospital in Sullivan, eight miles away. This was before I had a driver's license, but I had been driving around town and to the farm. As we were rushing down the road at least at legal speed or a little beyond, the ladies were concerned we would crash before she bled to death. Neither happened and she lived many more years, but without a portion of her hand and two fingers.

When the local postmistress decided to retire, Mom was hired into that position and the mailboxes were moved from the Post Office in the Barber Shop into the store. We became a one-stop grocery and post office with Mom running both.

Normally our tiny town was asleep by the time the TV news was off and the test pattern was displayed. However, one morning about 2:00am the phone rang. It was from across the street. A neighbor had been up studying when he heard a car stop and glass break. He peered outside to see someone moving around in our store. Appropriately, he called us. Dad and I grabbed our shot guns and met him and his brother in front of the house. We confirmed that the front door glass had been broken and that no one was in the store. As we were getting in the car, another car was coming and flashed its lights as it approached the store. We correctly surmised that it was the getaway car and was flashing its lights to inform the burglars that the pick-up car was on its way. We displayed our guns and the getaway car took off and turned toward Hutsonville, Illinois, leaving the burglars without a way home. We searched all the nearby buildings, including the fire house, but found no one. Soon the county sheriff arrived and took over the search. Ultimately, one of the perpetrators was found as he was trying to sneak back through the woods to cross the Wabash River back into Illinois. Unfortunately for him, he had broken through the ice on a creek and had frostbite on one of his feet. The sheriff took him to the hospital in the county seat. He gave up his buddies and they all spent some time in jail. His quick recovery may have been due to the hospital volunteer, Suzie Pirtle. Ironically, she was my girlfriend at the time. She said that he was handcuffed to the bed and she was cautioned by the nursing staff to not go into his room without them. While hardly a crazed felon, he did spend five years in jail for an empty-handed attempt at getting some cash. Once again, crime was proven to not pay.

Upgrading to the New House

As mentioned, Mom wanted a new house. She had been collecting designs and planning for several years. It was a dozen or so years from the time we moved into the old "classic" house until her plan was finalized. The new house would be all brick, three-bedroom, two bath and built immediately in front of the original house. It was so close that the front porch of the original house had to be removed before the new house could be built. We continued to live in the old house until the new house was ready for occupancy.

The new house was built in front of the old one. 1958

The old coal and kerosene stoves were replaced by electric heat installed in the ceiling. The sand plaster on the ceiling was smoothed over the wires in a circular pattern creating a finish that gave it an art work dimension. But there would be no air conditioning. Because it was an all-electric house, the house was awarded a Gold Medallion.

I was going to Purdue University during the time that the house was being built. But I did get home one summer to work on it. I even made one design change. I decided we could reduce the intrusion of the hot water heater in the second bathroom by turning the wall studs 90 degrees. However, the problem of unintended consequences resulted from the necessity to reduce the vent pipe diameter to fit in the thinner wall. We didn't realize the impact of that minor change until we found that the drains in that bathroom didn't drain as quickly due to the restricted vent. So much for the decisions of an aspiring engineer.

It wasn't a fancy house, but it was very functional, warm and secure. It had the joys and comforts of indoor plumbing, two bathrooms, separate bedrooms for each of us, and curb appeal. However, it didn't have air conditioning. Window fans continued to circulate the hot, humid air, along with the road noise.

Many of our neighbors were interested in the house and asked for a tour. We held an open-house and proudly guided them through each room, pointing out the distinctive design elements such as the built-in stereo cabinet and gun display case.

Chapter 3: School Days (A Big Fish in a Little Pond)

Graysville Consolidated School

Soon after arriving in Graysville, I was enrolled in the First Grade. The school was only a couple of city blocks from our house. But, in telling our boys of the trials of walking through the snow and up the hills, both ways, the distance seemed to grow over the years. That is until they visited in Graysville and saw the reality of how small the town and how short the walk.

Graysville Consolidated School.
All 12 grades were in the same building

Mom took me to school the first day and a teacher met me at the door. I started following that teacher only to be told I was headed the wrong way – perhaps a harbinger of days to come. Properly turned around and guided to the first-grade room, I was introduced to Miss Julia Burnett. One of the joys (?) of growing up in a very small community is that everyone knows everyone and most of everyone's business. It was no exception in school.

B.J.'s Favorite Picture of Me

Because the class sizes were small, both the first and second grades were in one room. Miss Burnett had been teaching the first and second grade for many years before and after I was in her classes. She knew how to handle first-graders. She was an institution unto herself. Scores of Graysville kids were introduced to school in her classroom.

I only have a few recollections of first grade. I wasn't very interested in quietly studying. Academically, I mastered the stories of Dick, Jane, and Spot and learned to write the alphabet in cursive. My social skills and interest in what my buddies were doing led to the embarrassment of having to take my little chair out into the hallway and sit there until I learned my lesson. Unfortunately, that lesson was neither quickly nor fully learned and that mode of punishment was awarded several times. I deserved my punishments.

Again, since the town was small, and my parents well known, Mom was always aware of my overly social exploits even before I got home. Consequently, there was additional correction upon my arrival in her presence as she explained the necessity of improving my academic skills and reducing my social activities.

Third and fourth grades were in the room next door. Being promoted from Miss Burnett's class meant moving up to Mrs. Dorothy Thompson's Third and Fourth Grade room. It seems that I was getting my act together because I only remember a trip or two to the Principal's Office and my grades were pretty good.

Further promotion brought moving to the next room down the hall with Mrs. Irma Monk teaching the Fifth and Sixth Grades.

In addition to the normal curriculum of reading, writing and arithmetic, we were very early introduced to music. Mrs. Vivian Church was the music teacher. In the lower grades we trooped down the hall to her room and learned to sing and read music. She had a special chalk holder that drew the lines of the scale evenly spaced across the backboard. She perfectly drew the treble clef and bass symbols and explained the music scale.

In Fifth Grade I joined band and chose the trumpet. Through Mrs. Church's tedious and persistent instruction and direction, I became rather proficient and a regular member of the band in Sixth Grade. I remember my first band concert. I had practiced and was ready. Mom and Dad bought me a new suit and Mom said I should polish my shoes. Nope, I didn't think the shoes needed polishing. As soon as I walked into the gym, Virginia Downs, who was a few years older, commented about how nice I looked, and I smiled. Then she said I should have polished my shoes. I was deflated, but I have never had ugly shoes since then. Shining shoes was one lesson that was learned long before the Air Force gave me the opportunity to perfect the process.

Mrs. Church was uncompromising. Individual practice was held in a small room off the stage in the gymnasium. Tapping my foot wasn't helping me to maintain the correct timing, so she jammed the point of her pencil into my leg with each beat. After several jabs in the same place, it began to hurt. Try as I might to inconspicuously move my leg to give that spot some rest, she somehow kept hitting the same target. Indeed, I got the point and timing improved. After the first chair graduated, I moved up to First Chair Trumpet in my sophomore year.

Each year our band joined with other school bands in our county for a concert held in the Sullivan High School Gym (our county seat). We practiced as an individual band for a couple of months. On the Friday before the big concert, we went to Sullivan and joined with the other bands to form one big band. There were break out trials with the guest conductor to determine the sequence of seating for each of the band sections. My Junior year, I placed second. Senior year I was awarded First Chair Trumpet in the County-wide Band.

Mrs. Church also staged a Christmas Musical every year. The entire school was somehow involved. There was the Rhythm Band with the youngest students dressed in uniforms melodiously banging musical sticks together as they marched around the gym. There was a program including scripted lines and performances. Parents helped by making costumes, setting up backdrops and marshalling the kids.

She also established choirs and musical groups. There was a boys' quartet for a couple of years, but when they graduated it was discontinued and I never had the opportunity to even try to sing. Perhaps it was because Mrs. Church had heard me in her music classes and decided I should stay with the trumpet.

A group of six girls sang beautiful harmonies and were very musically skilled. They became widely known as the G-Chords. Each of them was also in the band and choir. While I thought all of them were cute, one captured my attention.

Graysville "G-Cords" 1956-57

Vivian Church
Mary Nowlin, Sylvia Walker, Annetta Held
Suzie Pirtle, Sallie Medsker, Laconda Hayden

There were many important life-lessons from years in Mrs. Church's bands and programs. The first happened when I was in the first or second grade. I was given a speech to introduce the Christmas program. Mom drilled me until I had it down pat. However, when I walked out onto the stage for the dress rehearsal and saw all the school at my feet, I panicked. I couldn't say a word, nothing would come out. I ran off the stage only to be escorted back front and center. Nothing. I again ran off devastated and embarrassed in front of my friends.

After many years of Mom volunteering me for other speaking parts in school and in church, I lost some of the stage fright and became more confident. Since those halting attempts, I have become an accomplished speaker in front of large audiences, churches, and prestigious leaders. But the stage fright of seven decades ago still lingers. Other life-lessons included learning the value of practice, being on time, doing your best, being confident in front of people, as well as shining your shoes.

Back to the Books

Academics were never difficult for me and I was content to get through with mostly As and a few Bs. As I came to learn, the reason studies weren't difficult was because in the small school the academics were not as demanding as they should have been. The offered classes certainly exceeded state standards. However, mathematics topped out at introductory algebra and very basic geometry. There was no chemistry lab beyond a couple of demonstrated chemical reactions.

Mrs. Enid Monk was a very knowledgeable teacher of English. But I never learned all the conjugation of verbs and various nuances of the language. While these shortcomings never impacted my routine use of written and spoken language, they were manifested in studying English in college and in trying to learn a foreign language. Lack of vocabulary and sentence structure were also a challenge in college writing.

Mrs. Irma Gray was our History teacher. We used to joke that she was good in History because she was old enough to have lived most of it. There was some truth in that as my grandfather had hired her, and she had taught my dad. Regardless, she instilled a desire to learn more and provided a good basis for future classes and my USAF career.

Agriculture and Home Economics were also core courses at Graysville High School. The boys took shop and learned how to use saws and carpentry tools to build bird houses, tables and other useful items. We also learned how to raise and improve animal breeds. Seniors learned how to weld and work on cars. It is unfortunate that our society has become so technically oriented that TV advertisements make big jokes of a teenager's failure to know how to change a tire, so he must call his mom to have her send help.

Farm Shop was a practical, fun course.
My friend, Ed Cox, is repairing the sign

Another practical course was typing, learned by the touch method. After a couple of weeks, the letters on the key board were capped. Typing was the only high school class in which I got a D. Frankly I probably deserved to fail. However, I was on the basketball team and the coach's wife was the teacher. Had I failed I would have been ineligible to play basketball. Isn't it ironic that my lowest graded class is the one I use for hours every day? Today we call it "keyboarding".

Girls learned everything from cooking and baking to sewing. Many of them exhibited the products of their work at the 4-H fairs. As with men, women have been encouraged to go to college to learn technical skills and this is seen as being a much higher calling than Home Economics. It seems that maintaining the home and family has been out-sourced to nursery schools and drive through carry out.

I am a big supporter of girls who want to go to college and learn skills that will give them the opportunity to have careers outside the home. In my view, Motherhood is a woman's highest calling. But marriage and stay-at-home-mom isn't the only calling for every woman and our workplace has been much improved with addition of women.

My only direct influence with girls has been with our Favorite Granddaughter Brooke Watson; she quickly points out she is our only granddaughter. From the beginning, we have encouraged her to study hard, spend time to determine her gifts, and to pursue them with great vigor. She has more than met the challenge and we are justifiably very proud of her accomplishments. She is the quintessential achiever, straight As, music, horses, etc. She has completed her core courses and is pursuing the challenging studies to become a licensed Physical Therapist Assistant.

Basic life skills taught when I was in school are now seldom taught to either boys or girls and they suffer as they become adults. I have enjoyed teaching our boys basic car care and carpentry and their mom has enjoyed teaching them household tasks. As adults and dads, they are better at both carpentry and cooking than I was or am. Just as family around the dinner table was in my growing up, we were able to maintain it our family and we are very pleased that the lesson is continued with our children and their children. Family legacy and core values are best taught and learned around the family dinner table.

Moreover, not everyone should go to college. God gives all of us basic "leanings" that we need to understand and pursue. As I have repeatedly told our boys, you can be anything you want to be, but you must be good at what you choose. Dr. Martin Luther King Jr. specifically addressed this philosophy in a speech, "*What Is Your Life's Blueprint*". He encouraged the student audience to excellence and if street sweepers, to sweep streets as Michelangelo painted, Beethoven composed music, and Shakespeare wrote poetry such that all the Hosts of Heaven would welcome them as a great street sweeper who completed his work well. I wasn't as eloquent as Dr. King. I told them that if they were ditch diggers, their ditches should be the longest and straightest.

As school progressed from one class to the next, I assumed greater responsibilities in class governance and was usually the class vice president or president. It seemed that Jay Mike and I exchanged those offices over the years alternating depending on which of us held the office the year before.

Similar to Shop and Home Economics came 4-H and Future Farmers of America (FFA). I was active in both organizations with 4-H taking the priority. My 4-H involvement started with a few projects. As I grew, we added sheep, forestry, gardening, and other projects that were associated with our day-to-day lives. I was also on a state-wide livestock judging team with Sallie Medsker and Suzie Pirtle that won state championship competition with me being designated as the top judge of the competition. Success in these endeavors lead to being elected to local and county club offices. Thanks to Dana Nichols and Charlotte Phillips, I was appointed to the County Junior Leaders and moved up within that organization, becoming the president in my senior year.

High School Memories

Here are a few of the colorful memories of Graysville, school, 4-H and life on the farm.

Basketball was, and is, a really big deal in Indiana. Saturday discussions around the big stove in our store often centered on the high school team and its prospects for the year. If the team was good, everyone was happy. If it wasn't, there was lots of discussion about whether the coach should be fired, or the referees banished, or one of the guys on the bench should be starter. The Hollywood movie "Hoosiers" tells the story of the small Indiana town that won the Indiana state championship. It is very accurate. We watched the movie as a family and I could whisper to the boys what would happen next: dribbling while weaving through folding chairs, running up the school stairs at one end, down the hall and down the stairs at the other end, or layups. I took them back to the tiny gym in Graysville and I could see in their eyes the realization of the movie.

One of my memorable Christmas presents was my own basketball when I was about 8 years old. We played in friend's back yard or at an outdoor court at the school. Regardless of the venue, it was easy to get a couple of guys to play HORSE or even enough for a 3 on 3 game. Later, Uncle Gay built a regulation sized basketball backboard and goal and we mounted it on the coal house.

There was discrimination between the high school "A" and "B" Teams. The "B" (Junior Varsity) played in the first game and the two best guys got to move on as substitutes to the "A" (Varsity) game. You could quickly tell if a guy was on the "A" or "B" team by the color of his shoes. The "A" guys got white shoes and the school paid for them. But the "B" guys had to buy their own shoes and they had to be black high-tops. My playing in Freshman year was primarily on the "B" team and was upgraded to the bench on the "A" team most of the time. Sophomore year I made the "A" team and lettered in that and the following two years.

The Graysville Greyhound team wasn't a contender most years. A couple of years we won one or two games in the Sectional playoffs. No one on our team could dunk the ball and only a couple could even jump high enough to touch the rim. I wasn't very tall and played mostly as a point guard or forward.

There was one memorable game for me. I had misbehaved or something and wasn't allowed to start. Coach had me on the end of the bench away from him. However, with only a couple of minutes to play, our shooting forward fouled out of the game. Coach yelled at me and I went in with the Greyhounds down four points. First time down the floor, Larry passed me the ball and cut. I faked the handoff and released the jump shot, swish. On defense, I stole the ball and Larry and I ran down the floor, two-on-one just as we always practiced. Larry passed to me and I made the layup and was fouled. I sunk the free throw and we went ahead by one point. Again on defense with the clock running down to a couple of seconds, I stole the ball and held it until the horn sounded. We won. Two minutes of playing time, five points, and two steals. I was a hero, at least in my own mind and if for only one game.

Our band always played during the intermission between the "B" and "A" home games. I would play basketball on the "B" team. During the intermission, I would jump up on the stage and play in the band, then jump down and dress for the "A" team. The small school gave everyone the opportunity to do many things.

Other seasons brought other sports. We ran track and played baseball and softball. Since we had so few boys, every boy who wanted could make a team.

One of the great disadvantages of being such a small school was that we had no equipment beyond bats and balls. We ran track and played baseball in tennis shoes. There was no weight room or superior coaching. But it was good conditioning and lots of fun, especially the road trips.

Sitting and bored in afternoon study hall, I went to Jay Mike with an idea. Let's go talk to Coach. The Fifth and Sixth Grades are in recess at the same time and the gym is empty. If we volunteer to coach them during this period, we blow off study hall and get to go to the gym. He agreed, and we made our case to our coach. He took the plan to the principal and we were approved. We coached those grades for the next two years and were able to schedule some games with neighboring teams. It would be nearly 25 years later that I would coach another similar team, our son Derek's fifth grade team in Alabama.

Graysville School had a cafeteria with good home cooking. Lunch was always an enjoyable time of visiting with other students and filling our stomach with whatever the ladies of the kitchen prepared.

Cafeteria
Graysville School Cafeteria.

Earlier I mentioned Shop. If a boy was a junior or senior and enrolled in Shop, he was also on the Graysville Volunteer Fire Department. The single truck and one stall garage/fire house was immediately adjacent to school property. If the large siren on top of the firehouse was sounded during school hours, this group of boys responded, leaving class, running to the fire house, opening the door and jumping on the truck. Our janitor, Shy Shyrock, would be right behind us to drive the truck, siren screaming, to the fire. We knew how to operate the pump and hoses and were able to put water on the fire. Beyond that, there wasn't much we could do. Most of the fires were in barns and grass fires in the fields. We could handle those. Fortunately, only a few houses burned and there were no fatalities.

Top Row: Ronnie Walker, Gary Haydon, Danny Downs, Bill Bell, Clifford Clark, Mark Shipp.
Bottom Row: Everett Shryock, Terry McKinley, Melvin Forbes, Bill Coppage, Gary Kinnett, Larry Huff, Junior Meier, Dick Neal, Stephen Wible.

This picture is of the group the year after I graduated.

In addition to being a Volunteer Firemen, there were many other activities that we could enjoy in the farm environment that city kids would never imagine. Hunting was always a part of our activities. In the fall squirrels, quail, and rabbits were abundant on our farm. As the season approached Thanksgiving and Christmas, we hunted ducks and Canadian geese for our holiday dinners. Sometimes we hunted for predators that destroyed crops and animals. For a time, there was a bounty on groundhogs and foxes. Dad bought a Remington .222 with a scope specifically to deal with them. I used it often to reduce the hungry groundhogs that were causing a loss of our crops. Guns were part of our living on farms and hunting. It was not uncommon for guys to have gun racks over the back window of their pickup trucks. Often guns would be in cars and trucks in the school parking lot in order to speed getting to the hunting areas immediately after school.

One way the foxes were controlled was by a Fox Hunt. On a scheduled Saturday, a couple dozen men, boys, dogs and guns would meet at a designated farm where the foxes were causing problems. We would start the drive to force the foxes from their dens into open territory. Today in Texas, wild hogs are the menace. Perhaps we should form a Hog Hunt Program. I am certain that PETA would disapprove, but they disapprove of most things.

Years later I was home with B.J. and decided I should go squirrel hunting. She stayed in bed. When I returned home, I held the squirrel behind my back as I approached her. She was happy that I didn't harvest any, until I presented it. She still says that when I shot it, it fell into a creek and was frozen. Regardless, Mom fixed squirrel gravy for dinner; B.J. graciously declined.

Speaking of guns, we started early with BB guns. Bill saved his money to buy a pump BB gun. It arrived at the store and we had to give it a try. The pump mechanism was too hard for him so my friend or I would pump it then give it to him to shoot. Another friend was with us on this inaugural outing. He decided he would go home. On his departure, our friend turned around and said, "Yaa, Yaa, Yaa, bet you can't hit me." Jay Mike grabbed the gun, unconstrained by intelligence, pumped and fired as the challenger was about half way across the neighbor's yard. The little BB hit him in the back, and he fell like he was dead. We ran to him fearing the worst such as how will we tell his mom and our mom???? Fortunately, he only had a little blood blister, and he jumped up and ran home to tell his mom. I am sure there was a penalty to pay for both Bill and me when his mom called our mom.

There was another incident of serious absence of intelligence and good sense on my part, but never with a gun. Before I had a driver's license, I was driving around town and to the farm. In my early teens I would use the tractor to drive from our house to our farm, about 2 miles away. One day I invited Gary to go with me for an enjoyable day playing in our woods. I was driving the tractor and over controlling it down the road and Gary fell off. Thanks to God who protects children and fools, the tires were at their widest point to permit cultivating the row crops and he slid between them with only a little road rash. Tractors and kids don't mix well, and I was blessed that he wasn't hurt. The memory of what might have happened has stayed with me forever. I called him as I was writing this. He said he hadn't thought about it much, but that he did remember the incident. I again begged his forgiveness which he quickly gave.

Growing up on the farm also introduced me to interesting activities. A couple of years, several farmers got together to hire agricultural aerial applicators (crop dusters) to sow rye in the corn fields. By using the airplanes, the rye could be planted much earlier than by waiting until after the corn was harvested. On the arranged day, three WWI Stearman biplanes landed in Jim Kennett's south field. After a briefing of whose farm would be targeted, I drove to our farm and tied a red rag on the end of a cane fishing pole. I was instructed to stand at the end of the field and wave the flag for the pilot to line up on. After he passed over, still raining rye on my head, I moved over 10 rows and waited for his next pass. I loved the sound of those old round engines and the wind going through the wires and over the wings. Today, GPS and computers in sophisticated aerial application airplanes have replaced fishing poles and red flags and jet turbines have replaced old round, noisy engines.

As youngsters, we learned to work to earn a little spending money. I mowed yards, usually charging a dollar. I gave a discount to one widow and mowed her yard for several years for seventy-five cents. But Frosty Burton graciously paid $5.00 for his larger yard. We had other similar jobs, planting and harvesting watermelons, and working on other owner's farms. I worked a couple of summers driving a tractor for neighbors who paid $4.00 a day.

We picked sweet corn for Frosty. He had planted several acres and it had to be picked at exactly the right time. We selected the mature ears and passed over those that were not yet ready. A couple of pickings were required each year. My first year I drove the tractor pulling the wagon and the pickers walked along side throwing the ears into the wagon. The next year I moved to be a picker and Bill became the driver. With a couple of wagons full, we counted the ears and loaded them into one of his dump trucks to be taken to the Indianapolis market.

4-H was a great training ground

4-H was another opportunity to have fun and fellowship while doing our projects, raising the animals, preparing for the county fair, and holding both local and county meetings. 4-H prepared us for life. It gave us the opportunity to travel to other farms, enter judging contests, and even exchange students with a club in Wisconsin. We often got together to help each other prepare our animals and displays for the county fair. Leadership and challenging work were deeply imbedded in both 4-H and FFA. My experiences in those two organizations have been instrumental throughout my life and career.

The exchange with the Eau Claire, Wisconsin club was especially interesting. I arrived at the dairy farm on which I would stay at the same time the electricity went out. My host family had about 30 cows to milk manually. I told them I knew how to milk a cow, and I did. However, my skill couldn't keep up with their proficiency and they were completing the second cow while I was still on the first. Regardless, it was a great week including a barn dance in the loft of the host family's barn and fishing at their grandfather's lake. We froze some of the fish and I brought them back to Indiana where Mom fixed them for dinner.

A fellow 4-H member, Sallie Medsker, had the benefit of an older brother who had taught her to show sheep. She helped me to learn how to trim and block our lambs for show. Another big helper was John Patton. His dad, Oren, had a large farm and raised sheep. They both helped us prepare and show our sheep.

The Pattons taught me a valuable, enduring lesson. At one of the county fairs, John had won several first-place ribbons. One was for a "pen of lambs" which consisted of three lambs as equal as possible in looks, size, weight and confirmation. Only one of those lambs could be entered in Best of Show. Oren asked me to pick the one I thought would be a winner. I selected one and John showed it. It won. After the show, Oren said that he was giving me the lamb. I refused, then offered to pay for it. He explained that the reason he was giving it to me was because I could repay him by helping someone else in the future. That lamb became a member of our flock and produced great lambs for many years. It also encouraged me to help others when I had the knowledge and expertise. I also sponsored the Champion Aviation Award for the county fair many years after I had left Graysville and entered the Air Force.

One of the ways I helped in 4-H was in the preparation of other kids' lambs and sheep. I especially enjoyed helping the girl who lived across the road from our farm. It was always a pleasure when Suzie invited me to her house, ostensibly to help her with the sheep. She was also a cheer leader, played the trombone in the school band, sang with the G-Chords and we were on the same 4-H animal judging team. We were "Steadies" for most of our high school years and my first year of college. On dates, we often talked about what we wanted to be when we grew up. Of course, my topic was my desire to attend the Air Force Academy. She had other goals and our plans ultimately became mutually exclusive. After nearly four years of dating, she chose to pursue her life plan and I went on to attend The Academy. Fortunately, both of us accomplished our goals and have been blessed in our respective lives and families. Through a school reunion and Facebook, we have been able to fill in the blanks and cheer each other's successes.

Our township was Turman, named after early settlers in the area. About the time of Prohibition or a little later there was a dance hall near the school. At some point, it was purchased and converted into a community use building named the Turman House. We held our 4-H meetings and other social events there. On a couple of Saturday nights a month, neighbors would bring out their guitars, banjoes and assorted instruments and square dances were held. It was a great place for boys and girls to meet and learn to dance under the watchful eye of parents who also enjoyed square dancing. The Turman House continued into the 21st Century.

The lessons of sharing and community involvement have continued throughout my lifetime. While I haven't had lambs to bestow on anyone, I have repaid the Oren Patton debt several times over by helping other people. The mechanism has varied to teaching flying, helping where needed and serving in the church. When we built our current house, we added a Casita, a bedroom and bath off the entrance courtyard. It has been used by dozens of family, friends and others who were visiting us or needed a place to stay. One dear friend's house burned, and they spent their first night with no home with us. On separate occasions we have given two college girls a room when they didn't have the money for an apartment. A couple who have a ministry of Bible training for pastors in Kenya, stayed with us nearly three months while their new house in our neighborhood was being completed.

I graduated from high school in a class of 16, all were close friends; most of us had been through the entire 12 years together.

My Graduating Class of Graysville High School, 1958

Church Was Always Important

My parents were committed to attending church as a family. Soon after I was born, they had me baptized in the Methodist Church in Hammond. When we moved to Graysville, there was a Methodist Church on the same intersection as our store. We became regular members and attended every Sunday for Sunday School and church.

Graysville Methodist Church where I accepted Jesus as my Savior. It sits on the crossroads of the only roads in town.

Sunday School with my buddies was always a challenge for our teachers. Leo Phillips and Emma Cox persevered over the years and were instrumental in preparing us to accept Christ as our personal Savior. While there were diversions from the straight path, the seeds that were planted there have grown and blossomed over the years to a greater commitment to serve Him.

Church also provided leadership training through Christmas and Easter plays and the Methodist Youth Fellowship (MYF). We were encouraged to lead younger members in Bible Studies and develop our group's plans for extended service to those outside of the church. I will be eternally thankful for the little church in Graysville. From my first commitment to Christ there, to years of trying to follow Biblical standards and His leading, to recently being baptized in the Jordan River, I continue to press forward to the mark of the high calling of Jesus Christ.

Confronted with Academic Reality (1958-1960)

4-H and my artificially high grades led to a scholarship to Purdue University. I was immediately introduced to my academic shortcomings. There were more guys in my dorm cube than the total of only 16 boys and girls in my high school graduating class. In fact, there were more students in my Freshman Chemistry lecture class than the total population of my home town, Graysville. Reality was quick and brutal.

Physics was an introduction to the challenges of understanding the spoken English of my American lecturer, Chinese lab instructor, and Indian classroom instructor. Trying to understand them explaining the laws and application of physics was well beyond my comprehension. I even tried tutoring from the upper classmen in the dorm, but with little success. I enrolled in the summer session hoping that the smaller classes would help. While grades improved, when averaged with the year before, I was still shy of the 2.0 grade point average necessary to stay enrolled. The good news was that based on the upward trajectory, I was placed on probation and allowed to enroll in the fall semester. When those grades failed to overcome the terrible Freshman year, I met an academic board and was given the opportunity to take my academic pursuits elsewhere.

It was extremely embarrassing and humiliating to call Dad to come get me and be disenrolled at Purdue. We had never known anyone to flunk out of college. In one of the ironies of life, several years later the Dean of Purdue University was on the board that selected me to be one of the Outstanding Young Men of America.

One of Dad's high school classmates was the Registrar at Indiana State and one of his brothers, Carlos, was a professor there. A couple of calls and I was registered for the Spring Semester at Indiana State.

Dad was still working in Terre Haute, only a few miles from the college. I moved back home and commuted every day with him. I retook several of the classes from Purdue and was able to get some decent grades. I enjoyed the time with Dad and his co-riders for the thirty minutes each way to and from Terre Haute. But I wasn't enjoying Indiana State.

In an attempt to get my grades up, Uncle Carlos spoke to the head of the evaluation department. In my free time I would go to the evaluation office and take tests that were never graded. The grade wasn't the objective. Rather, learning how tests are constructed, how to take them, how to manage the time available, and how to make educated guesses became the goal. It was very helpful. I did learn much about testing and used that knowledge in taking the tests to qualify for the Air Force Academy – my third attempt.

Chapter 4: First Step Toward the Wild Blue Yonder

Off to the Air Force Academy (1960-1964)

I first applied to The Academy in my senior year of high school. In filling out the application, I was impressed with my accomplishments. I was near the top of my class, had good grades, had an athletic history, and was well rounded with band and 4-H. However, the last question was like a pin bursting my ego balloon, "How many were in your graduating class?" Entering the number 16 summed up my "Big Fish in a Small Pond" status. I wasn't accepted and reluctantly began my "Plan B" by enrolling at Purdue University.

I applied a second time the following year. Another rejection letter came. I remember Dad delivering it to me when I was on a tractor in the field. Heartbroken with two rejections. I was not doing well at Purdue and had worked summers at the Sullivan County Rural Electrification Membership Corporation as an apprentice electrician. My ambition was beyond that level, but my skills were not. I just didn't see a path forward for the long haul.

Rejected and dejected from The Academy and not doing especially well in college, I was resolute to "forget those things which are behind and reach forth to those things which were before". (Philippians 3:13 with minor editing). I submitted a third application to The Academy.

Whether my extra year of college had improved my qualifications and test scores, or they were tired of reading my applications, this time I was accepted. The third time and persistence were charm for me. In the middle of the semester at Indiana State I was in a chemistry lab when Uncle Carlos came to pull me out of class. He told me that Mom had called, and I had received a telegram from the United States Air Force Academy informing me that I had been selected to enter the Class of 1964. However, I had to respond immediately. After talking to Uncle Carlos for a moment, I left my Bunsen Burner blazing with my lab partner, ran to the Terre Haute House Hotel, and sent an acceptance telegram. My interest in pursuing the classes at Indiana State quickly waned as I worked to be ready to go to The Academy in June.

I was on my way toward the plan that I believe God had placed in me long ago. In June 1960 I left Graysville for the first step toward the Wild Blue Yonder. My first commercial airline flight was in a DC-3 with a change in Chicago on the way to Colorado Springs. My last night as a civilian was spent at the Acacia Hotel across the street from a beautiful park and near the Methodist Church that I would later attend.

Arising early, I got on the bus to The Academy and began in-processing. The sergeant there told me I could sit and wait before stepping out the door. I replied that I was ready. I wasn't and had no clue as to what would await as soon as I opened that door.

With a small bag in hand and a tag around my neck listing my new service number, squadron and room assignment, I entered a world that was distinctly different from the farm in Graysville. I was becoming a member of the Class of 1964, only the sixth class to enter the Academy. Fewer than 2500 had entered The Academy before me. The first class graduated only a year before I entered.

Upper Classmen were ready, even though I was not. I immediately learned how to stand at attention, run my chin to the back of my neck and "Hit It" for pushups. Freshmen at The Academy are called "Doolies." Introduction to being one was eye-opening.

Fortunately, since I was an early one, the arrival of more buses and guys diverted the Upper Classmen from me to the new victims coming out of the door from the in-processing room. I was ushered to the supply room and my arms were filled with uniforms, underwear, boots and shoes. I was then escorted to my room and told to start unpacking the newly issued supplies and to arrange my room to the strict requirements of the instructions on my bed. As I was finishing that task and sitting on the bed, a new kid came in the door. I stood to introduce myself and he immediately turned pale thinking I was an Upper Classman ready to jump all over him. It took a while to calm him down and explain that I was his classmate and roommate.

At the end of our first day, for our introduction to The Academy, we assembled in one of the large lecture halls. The Superintendent, a three-star Air Force General, welcomed us. Beginning his comments, he asked those who were in the top 5 percent of their high school class, those who lettered in more than one sport, those who were officers in their class, etc., to stand. In no time, everyone was standing. Even more quickly than at Purdue, I realized that I was now a very small fish in a very big ocean and the sharks were on patrol. As we were told to sit, he said to look at the guys on each side of us and that one wouldn't be there at graduation. He was about right. Of the 772 that were in that room, 498 of us graduated, about one-third did not.

Doolie Summer, as it is called, is a time of preparation. The new class receives instruction on The Academy, the Honor Code and military history. The Honor Code is the basis of The Academy and the Air Force. *"We will not lie, cheat or steal, nor tolerate among us those who do."* It was not difficult for me because the Watson family and the small town of Graysville operated that way, every day.

Physical conditioning is another thrust of the summer. We ran everywhere. Pushups were issued for any and all infractions, regardless of how minor. We were led in exercises in the dormitory hallway before we had our evening showers. Even breathing was a challenge since we were at over 7000 feet above sea level. The combined effect of physical exercise and altitude quickly developed our bodies to be able to withstand the rigor of the soon to start academic year.

Competitive games were played *"on the fields of friendly strife are sown the seeds that on other days and other fields would bear the fruits of victory."* This is a quote from General Douglas MacArthur that we had to learn from a small book that we carried everywhere. *"Contrails"* contained a whole encyclopedia of quotations, airplane facts, and "Knowledge" that we had to memorize. Now, more than 58 years later, many of those quotations and facts can be instantly recalled even though I am challenged trying to remember what I had for dinner last night. Many of the tests to determine our comprehension and recall of the facts in *Contrails* were administered by upper classmen at the table during each of the meals. A wrong answer brought the order to "Sit Up" and stop eating. Hunger is a great motivator.

Thanks to the two years spent at Purdue and Indiana State, I was much better prepared to enter the academic challenge of The Academy. I have been often and thankfully reminded that had I been selected the first two years that I applied, I would not have been adequately prepared to complete The Academy course. Failing out of The Academy would have been much more painful and life altering than failing out of Purdue had been.

Because of the transfer of prior college credits, I wrongly allowed the academic advisors to put me into advanced classes in math and chemistry, classes that had been hard in the civilian colleges. I finished two years of math in my first year and two semesters of chemistry in one semester. Unfortunately, my grades suffered. While I was above passing, my grade point average took a hit. As the inscription on the Eagle and Fledglings Statue says, *"Man's flight through life is sustained by the power of his knowledge."* For us cadets, it was sustained by the power of our GPA and mine wasn't great.

In January it was announced that we would be marching in the parade for the inauguration of our new president, John F. Kennedy. The Air Force staged a practice deployment of C-130s to carry the entire cadet wing to Washington. However, the East Coast weather didn't cooperate. It began a snow storm of epic proportions about the time the first airplanes arrived at Andrews AFB. The airplanes carrying my squadron were on final approach when Andrews went below landing minimums and we diverted to Langley AFB in southeastern Virginia. The airplanes that hadn't started the approach were diverted to an airbase in Tennessee. Again, the Air Force came through with busses to take those of us at Langley the rest of the way to Washington. A trip that should take less than four hours took more than 12. We were to be housed in old dormitories at Fort Belvoir just south of D.C.

Unfortunately, the soldier that was to build the coal fire in my barracks went AWOL. When we arrived after midnight, there was no heat and the showers were freezing cold. We got a little sleep, then dressed in the warmest clothes and big horse-blanket style overcoat. It continued snowing until about the time we headed to the parade. Of course, the parade was running late by an hour or more while we stood in the open. Snow was several inches deep on the parade route. But we made it and can say that we marched for the JFK Inauguration.

We were able to spend the next couple of days in Washington. The first night a girl from my hometown who was living in D.C. arranged for several of her girlfriends to meet us for a short party at her apartment, but we had to be back to Fort Belvoir by midnight. The next night, our classmate Fred Gregory, later to become a Space Shuttle pilot and acting director of NASA, invited us to his parents' home. It was a great evening and his parents are still talking about how much pizza and beer were consumed in a few hours.

Marching in JFK's Inaugural Parade was a highlight of our Doolie (Freshman) year. Three years later we marched to lunch to be informed of President Kennedy's assassination. The optimism of 1960 was replaced by the hatred and evil of 1963.

My academic achievement increased over the first year and I did reasonably well until I hit German my sophomore year. The first semester I passed with a "D", but the second semester fell below the mark. There was a mechanism to take a second final exam that if passed, gave you a "D." After lots of tutoring, I took the test. As I was taking the test, I could hear the USAF Thunderbirds Aerial Demonstration Team flying over the parade field. I doubled-down and thankfully passed. However, I have always wondered if I really passed or my professors, both Air Force officers, thought that I had talents in areas that wouldn't require me to speak German and they wanted me out of their foreign language department. Regardless, I completed my sophomore year burdened with 10 hours of "D" against my GPA. Ironically, I was stationed three years in Germany and have many

German friends. My command of the language isn't much better now than it was when I was slightly above failing many years ago.

The summers between the academic years were full. Our first summer field trip between our freshman and sophomore years was to USAF, Army, and Navy bases around the U.S. The highlight was flying in the back seat of an F-100F and going supersonic. I was hooked. I wanted to be a fighter pilot and committed everything within my power to achieve that goal. The AF also put on a firepower demonstration right in front of us. It was awesome. Bombs were exploding, cannons were firing, and an F-104 fired a missile then shot it down with a second missile. An assault landing by a C-123 resulted in a blown tire and the airplane sliding off the very narrow, rough landing strip right before our eyes. The Navy took us on a cruise out of San Diego. The Army took us to Fort Benning and demonstrated their tanks and artillery. That field trip further convinced me that I had made the right choice to Go Air Force.

I gave up some of my summer vacation to return to Fort Benning to complete the Army Airborne School and earn the silver Army Parachutist Wings. Being gung-ho Air Force Academy cadets, we had to brag about it with our Army jump instructors. They are rightfully very proud of their service and had a "Follow Me" statute with full combat gear and his hand forward as leading the fight. The night after our first jump we put a diaper on him and hung a yoyo from his finger. We also slid pillow cases over the jump towers that were topped with signs reading "AIRBORNE." By just painting two letters on the pillow cases, we converted the signs to read "AIRFORCE." We also painted our helmets Air Force Blue and affixed a decal of a falcon under a parachute. The next morning, we learned that the instructors were not happy and didn't appreciate our attempt at good, clean fun. After administering the maximum push-ups and other punishment, they threaten to expel our entire class. However, after some negotiation between our leadership and the administration, they allowed us to complete the jumps and qualified all of us "Airborne."

Between the sophomore and junior years summer trips were to overseas bases. Cadets who had taken Spanish that year went to Latin America. If you took German or a European language, you went to Europe. My German "qualification" (?) allowed me to go to Spain, Italy, France, and Germany. We visited and received briefings at military bases and U.S. Embassies which gave us intimate insight into day-to-day military and diplomatic activities during the Cold War.

The summer before our senior year was the best. We went to an Air Training Command base and were introduced to pilot training. I went to Craig Air Force Base in Selma, Alabama. We went through a short T-37 course of academics and flight training. I did very well, and my instructors wanted to allow me fly solo. But The Academy disapproved because it would then change from a flight introduction to a flight training program.

Being the Senior Class, we returned to The Academy to conduct the Doolie Summer program for the incoming Freshman class. The Academy mission is to train leaders. Our leadership of the new class was instrumental in developing our leadership skills and was core to the entire Academy program. Rather than being the Doolie on the receiving end of correction as I had been three years earlier, I was now correcting and training the new guys coming into the Class of 1967.

Athletics were a major portion of our Academy experience. Of course, intercollegiate sports dominated. However, not all of us could qualify at that level. Intramural sports were required for the rest of us. Given that most of us were multiple letter winners in high school sports, intramural athletics were demanding. During my four years I played in many sports that I had never played and some I had never seen. Soccer was one of those that I knew about but had not played. Water polo, field hockey, and lacrosse were new to me. Somehow, I was able to play and contribute to our squadron's success in all the sports.

In a rugby game (another sport I had never seen) during my junior year, I was clipped as I was kicking the ball. My left knee was taken out and I went to The Academy hospital. This unfortunate injury became a blessing. The daughter of an AF officer also was at the hospital in the orthopedic surgery ward. She had damaged her knee in a skiing accident. Because she was the dependent of an active duty Air Force member, she could be admitted to the hospital and receive the same care that we received. Orthopedics were at the top of The Academy Hospital's skills. I met Jan while roaming of the halls on crutches trying to get my knee to work. The day of my operation, the doctors decided against putting her through surgery to avoid the ugly scars on her pretty legs, so she was put in a cast instead. They weren't as concerned about me having a scar, and it is a big one even today.

I was the last of seemingly a dozen surgeries that day. After much effort, they were able to give me a spinal block for the surgery. Returning to my room with no control of anything south of my waist, nature took over to release the fluid built up during surgery. Having no clean pajamas, the nurses decided to put me back into bed as Jan came hobbling into the room on her new crutches. The nurses attempted to protect my dignity and pulled the sheet up to my chest. Accompanying her was her very cute roommate dressed in a Braniff Airways uniform. My introduction to Bette Jayne Douglas, or B.J. as she preferred, was brief. I remember her being very attractive. She remembers me as being pale white with hairy armpits being fully displayed with my hands locked behind my head. She also remembers being hungry from having worked all day as a Braniff reservationist and that I was offered a milk shake. When I asked the nurse to save it for me, she was ready to ask if she could have it. While I didn't feed her then, we have been eating together for more than half a century.

I developed excuses to see her a couple of times during the second semester of my junior year. When I returned to The Academy in the summer of my senior year, we started dating. As the school year progressed, so did our relationship. We began spending any free time together. Dances at Arnold Hall, The Academy social center, double dates with classmates and their girlfriends, and other reasons to be together became the goal.

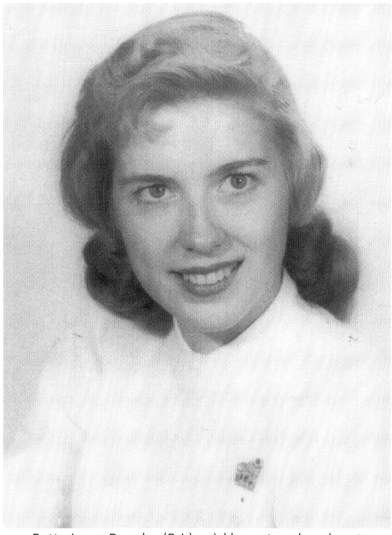

Bette Jayne Douglas (B.J.) quickly captured my heart

When I had a pass for an overnight, I spent it with her family sleeping on the sofa bed in their home that was close to the Academy.

George and Virginia Douglas (and Pierre)
B.J.'s parents

In the fall of 1963, I gave her a pin as a token of my increasing love for her and the talk of marriage became serious. Because we met at The Academy and her involvement in my life there, I wanted her to have a miniature of my class ring as an engagement ring. She had been an integral part of my Academy life and I wanted her to have a token of that experience. I ordered it from the same company that manufactured my ring and had a small diamond set into its crown. It arrived just in time for Valentine's Day. Having received her father's blessing, after enjoying a lovely dinner, I got down on one knee and asked her to marry me. Her acceptance was joy in my life.

Our first inclination was to delay getting married for six months until the Christmas after graduation to permit me to go to pilot training and her to continue to work for Braniff. Soon it was obvious that we should start both our personal lives and our professional careers together. Moreover, we didn't want to wait any longer. The wedding date was set for the day after graduation.

Since our wedding would be in the new, beautiful Academy Chapel, we didn't have much to do to set it up. Interestingly, our class was the first class that could be married in the recently completed chapel. Four classmates were married the day of graduation, but we waited until the next day. B.J. and her mother were scrambling to make all the arrangements. B.J. was able to take her mother on Braniff to Dallas for a special mother-daughter time and to pick out her mom's wedding dress. I am glad they had that time together as our Air Force lives never placed us near them. They did a marvelous work in arranging the details in only a few months. Mom would have loved to participate, but the distance from Indiana to Colorado Springs kept her from being closely involved. B.J. and Mom talked on the phone often making Mom feel involved in the process and wedding.

Graduation and Wedding in Two Days (June 3 and 4, 1964)

June Week is a flurry of graduation activities. There were dances, parades, parties and ceremonies. Mom and Dad had never met B.J. and were committed to coming to the graduation and wedding. B.J. and I made all the arrangements for their visit. Coincidently, we had just finished the reservations for them at the motel as they drove up. I know Mom would have preferred the opportunity to freshen up before meeting B.J. for the first time. The introductions in the parking lot weren't formal, but they were warm and inclusive. Brother Bill, Uncle

Gay and Aunt Jeanette, Uncle Carlos and Cousin Bud, and Laurel and Fern Whitman from home accompanied them for the festivities.

With family and friends in town, everything moved at a fast pace. The day before Graduation Day opened with dense fog all around The Academy, especially at the Parade Grounds. The band led the Cadet Wing down the ramp from the academic area and onto the grounds. The family and others in the stands could hear the music, but they couldn't see anyone. They could only imagine that we were on our way. As the ceremony proceeded, the Cadet Wing Officers went forward. As they progressed toward the reviewing stands, first their feet, then their waists, finally their heads began to emerge from the fog and the crowd started cheering. The ceremony continued, and the parade was completed.

In the afternoon after the parade, we had a wedding rehearsal at the Cadet Chapel. Chaplain Shoemaker, the Methodist Chaplain, would marry us. It was an assembly line process since many of my classmates were being married there as well. The rehearsal was quick, and I didn't remember all the things I was supposed to do. After the rehearsal we moved from the Chapel to the traditional Rehearsal Dinner at B.J.'s parents' house. The dinner was very informal and was extremely well done. B.J.'s mother and grandmother made it perfect in every way. It was the first opportunity for our parents to get to know each other.

The Graduation Ceremony was held on June 3, 1964 in Falcon Stadium with parents and friends in the stands and we graduating seniors on the field. Our names were called in our class graduating order of merit, with mine being toward the end. Regardless of the sequence, I was graduating. We walked across the stage, accepted our diplomas and commissions as Second Lieutenants and we saluted our classmate who was immediately in front of us. Returning to our chairs, we waited with great anticipation, *"Gentlemen, you are dismissed."* With that iconic phrase, we threw our hats in the air and the Air Force started the flyby of each of the diverse types of aircraft we would be learning to fly. While I loved the fighters, Dad was most impressed with the U-2 that climbed in a circle right over the stadium until it was out of sight. B.J.'s mom liked the big B-52.

My graduation picture.

The Family at Graduation
B.J. on my left
Mom and Dad to my right.
Brother Bill and Uncle Gay behind B.J., Cousin Bud to my far right

Our wedding day (6.4.64) was extremely busy. I went to the weddings of a couple of my classmates in the morning while B.J. was getting prepared with her parents and bridal attendants. Her Matron of Honor was her older sister, Barbara. Also standing with her was Jan, her former roommate who had introduced us, and another of her high school friends. Brother Bill was my best man and my roommate, John Jacobs, and another classmate, Mike Holcomb, stood with me. Barbara's son, Jeff, was the ring bearer and B.J.'s friend's daughter was the Flower Girl.

The Cadet Chapel is an impressive edifice with its spires and stained-glass windows reflecting God's glory and presence. B.J. said the aisle was even longer from her perspective. She was radiantly beautiful as she began her walk on her Dad's arm. I was overwhelmed by her beauty and presence and the environment. Somehow, I stammered through our vows and the ceremonial kiss and we headed back down that aisle as husband and wife. She stopped to kiss her mom and dad and I said goodbye to my parents. Leaving the chapel several of my squadron mates had formed the traditional sabre tunnel of honor as we descended the steps.

We were married in The Academy Chapel

Husband and Wife, Finally

Squadron Mates Provided the Sabre Salute Sendoff

I could not have been happier. Several classmates came by the reception to extend their best wishes. Don Hall had been a roommate and came with his new wife, Liz. B.J. and I had double-dated with them. We paid for the reception using most of our cash and ran to our car. It was a 1964 Ford Galaxy, with stick shift and no air conditioning, to begin our honeymoon on the way to pilot training in Selma, Alabama. We elected to not have car air conditioning and were headed to Alabama. What were we thinking?

Many years later we were in Colorado with our two boys and their wives and wanted to give them a tour of The Academy and the Chapel. As we approached the chapel door, we were intercepted by a wedding planner who said we couldn't go in. I quietly explained that we just wanted to show our family where we were married. She insisted, then I insisted. B.J. and I started walking down the aisle with the wedding planner screaming at us. We got half way, turned around to check on our family, and they were out of the door, totally embarrassed. They still enjoy telling people about the time they were thrown out of the USAF Academy Chapel.

We didn't travel very far. We went to Denver for our first night together. We had a lovely dinner at Trader Vic's and headed to our room. Before we got into bed, we knelt at the bedside and committed our marriage to the Lord. At our encouragement, our boys did the same on their wedding nights. B.J. and I have been praying together every night since that first night and the Lord has indeed blessed our marriage of more than a half-century.

Waking with my new bride was a wonderful experience. We were finally together and headed off to a future we could only imagine. Filled with excitement, we started the trek to Craig Air Force Base, with a stop for the night in Dallas and a few days of honeymooning in New Orleans. New Orleans was great. We did all the touristy things like Brennan's, Court of Two Sisters, tour of the old homes and the Mississippi, and Café du Mond with beignets for breakfast. We had one minor mishap. With the stress of the previous week and the drive, we were tired and ready to relax. Being very pale from the Colorado winter, we decided we needed some sun. We relaxed by the pool and slept for far too long. The resulting sunburn required innovative togetherness that night. Stories of our honeymoon in New Orleans may have influenced Derek and Kelly to honeymoon there as well. After a couple of days enjoying each other and New Orleans, we continued to pilot training in Selma, Alabama.

Eager to introduce my new wife to my early childhood and hoping cooler weather was in Indiana, we finished renting the apartment and drove to Graysville. Mom and Dad hosted a reception for us at Uncle Gay's house. Many friends, our family, and several of my high school classmates attended. It was a proud moment to introduce B.J. She was very gracious and enjoyed meeting them.

Uncle Gay and Aunt Jeanette left the next day for Ecuador where Uncle Gene was serving with the USAID. They kindly offered their house to us for privacy, if we would feed their cats. B.J. quickly agreed, missing my signals to her to be cautious. Aunt Jeanette had about 40 cats living around the barns, under the house and who knows how many other places. Aunt Jeanette took us to an old building where cat food was stored from floor to ceiling. She explained that we should take a bucket of the dry food and several cans of food to the trough she had made from an old tractor tire and tarpaulin. She said to dump it all in the middle, put some on the concrete near the pump house and in another pan, then go back into the house. She explained that the cats wouldn't come out if we were visible. Completing our chore, we retreated to the house and peeked out of the windows. Immediately there was an invasion of cats from every corner of the compass and from under every building. They quickly surrounded and devoured the food, then retired to their hiding places.

Uncle Gay had an old WWII jeep. I suggested we should crank it up and tour some of the places that were special to me, including The Round Barn. It worked well until we were several miles into the Wabash River bottoms when it decided to die and wouldn't restart. B.J.

enjoyed the stories, but her fun meter was pegged with the bouncing around farm roads. When the jeep died, she turned and looked at me as if to say, "What now farm boy? You have me miles from anywhere in a relic jeep that just quit running."   As I looked across a nearby field, I saw a farmer and tractor working the field. I told her I would go to him and he would give us a ride home. As I approached him, I recognized that it was a good friend. He did come over and help us restart the jeep. But he has totally enjoyed telling the story that it was the first time a married couple had used the excuse of automobile trouble to park in the river bottoms.

While we enjoyed our week in Indiana, both of us were ready to head back to Alabama and start pilot training. And, we left with the agreement that returning to the farm wasn't in either her or my plan for the future.

Entering pilot training and what became an Air Force career was the last step away from being the Farm Boy.

Chapter 5: A New Wife and a New Life

Our First Duty Assignment: Finally, at Pilot Training (1964-1965)

A friend who had graduated one year ahead of me and his wife, a close friend of B.J.'s, had preceded us to Selma. They were very kind and found us an apartment; well, it was sort of an apartment. Story Apartments was singularly designed for student pilots for their one-year tour at Craig AFB. It was a few miles east of the base on the road that would become internationally known as the road of the Dr. Martin Luther King Jr. march from Selma to Montgomery.

Mr. & Mrs. Story had a large plantation style home. They split it down what was formerly a large center hallway. They lived on the left side. We rented the right side consisting of the half hallway as a living room, a large master bedroom and small bath and a kitchen with eat-in area. There was a small screened-in porch.

Our starting monthly Air Force salary $222.40 plus $47.88 for subsistence (food) and about $80 for rent. We thought we were in the big bucks when I started flying and collecting an extra $100 per month hazardous duty pay. It was a huge reduction from B.J.'s salary at Braniff.

Starting a home from scratch with that paltry income was a challenge, but B.J. was up to the task. We found furniture at Railroad Salvage, it didn't take much for our little place. We also found a street in Selma that was only one block off the main drag. The stores there were much less expensive, and we found what we needed. When we told Mr. Story of our find, he was appalled. We had shopped in an area normally used only by Blacks. We had been ignorant of the deep prejudices in the South and this was 1964. The animosity was about to boil over, and we were there to witness history being made.

One of the joys of payday, besides being able to pay the bills, was a stop at a very dirty road side BBQ stand. They started on Thursday burning the oak logs into charcoal so that by Friday they were ready to begin making BBQ and Brunswick Stew. The heavy smoke and BBQ smells permeated the entire area. The odor was enticing as we drove by, but we were reticent to stop because of the appearance. Mr. Story assured us that it was safe. After one bite, we had a new favorite payday pastime, stopping for a BBQ sandwich and fries.

After a few months at Story Apartments, we had the opportunity to move onto Craig Air Force Base in a nice two-story, two-bedroom duplex shared with another student pilot and family a class or two ahead of us. Being on base gave me the opportunity to ride a bike to class and the flight line, avoiding the need for a second car.

One couple in our class was from Indiana. At the introductory meeting he and I saw each other and thought we had known each other before. We talked for a moment and then remembered the connection. He had grown up in Terre Haute, about 25 miles from me, and we had been together in Air Force ROTC at Purdue. He was commissioned through the Indiana Air National Guard and would return to Indiana to fly after pilot training. John and Mary Beth Thomas are still close friends even though they now live in North Carolina and we are in Texas.

Mary Beth worked for the General Manager of the Albert Hotel which was segregated. We were at a small party at the hotel the night before Dr. King was going to try to register there. I asked the manger what he was going to do. He quickly replied, "I am going to meet Dr. King at the door and personally welcome him and register him." He further said it was time for segregation to end, and all of us agreed. True to his word, he and Mary Beth registered Dr. King the next morning.

The entire story of the March from Selma to Montgomery hasn't been well told. There was an earlier attempt. When the marchers crossed the Edmund Pettis Bridge from the city into the county, they were met with sheriff deputies, dogs, cattle prods and tear gas. We heard the developing news on the radio and drove from the base to the location. Upon arriving, most of the people had dispersed, but tear gas cannisters were all over the road and the smell of the gas remained. It was immediately obvious that we should not be there and quickly drove across the center island and headed back on the base. Had that march not been turned back, the marchers would have had a very difficult time. It was a busy highway, some of it through a swamp. A couple of days later there was a freezing rain that would have caused great challenges for the marchers. It is questionable whether the march would have succeeded or have been lost in the hardships of that week.

President Johnson saw the TV and press reports of the first march being turned back into town by hatred and violent force. He acted by sending in the National Guard and support operations. When the second march was scheduled, C-130s brought in kitchens, food, shelter and other provisions onto Craig AFB. The Army troops bedded in our base gym and used other base facilities. When Dr. King arrived with his group, the west bound portion of the highway between Selma and Montgomery had been closed and the east bound section used for two lane traffic. The Army had set up hot food, shelter, first aid, and other facilities for the marchers. And, the weather was much warmer with no rain.

This second march began on a Sunday afternoon. We stood on the base and saw Dr. King and the marchers start what would be the battle that won integration. Watching them in column pass by on the other side of the highway, we were appalled by the hatred displayed by people driving by with vile signs on their vehicles and shouting vulgarities. It was a scene that has affected us for a lifetime.

Finally, Pilot Training Begins

We came to Selma and Craig Air Force Base to learn to fly. I had been there the previous summer for the introduction to pilot training program. This was the real thing. This was the first step on what would become a twenty-six-year career.

The First Step into the First Cockpit
More than 56 years of stepping into cockpits has followed

I had hoped to get my previous instructor, but he was assigned to another squadron. Unfortunately, I drew another who could be one of the meanest and most sarcastic guys on the planet. It seemed that he came to work angry and just got more upset as the day wore on.
To say that my instructor and I didn't hit it off would be a woeful understatement. He seemed to resent that I had done well in the introduction program there the summer before and ridiculed any mistake that I made. His constant berating was not positive and affected me both in the air and on the ground, even at home. He also had a grudge against Academy graduates.

There were four or five of us assigned to each instructor pilot and we sat at his table in the briefing room. Ken, John, Lee and I were at one table and he treated all of us the same. In return, all of us had the same opinion of him. His negative influence was so great that he could turn a good day into a nightmare. We didn't fly every day. On a non-fly day, Lee would come in happy and in a positive mood. Unfortunately, if the schedule changed and Lee was assigned to fly with our instructor, his mood would immediately change in the opposite direction. Occasionally in the worst of times, he would get up from the table; go to the bathroom and vomit before the flight.

John bore the brunt of his demeaning attitude. He failed a couple of check rides and was forced to meet a Flying Evaluation Board that would determine if he would continue in pilot training or be washed out. John asked me to testify as to our instructor's teaching ability and behavior. One of the colonels on the board asked me, "Does your instructor's behavior affect you after you leave the base?" I replied, "Yes. Sometimes I go home angry and downtrodden and it affects my home life." There were no smiles in the room. Unfortunately, based on John's marginal performance in both the air and in academics, he was washed out of pilot training, but went on to graduate from navigator training. Upon completing his USAF commitment, our instructor resigned and became a pilot for Delta Airlines.

On one flight with him, I was having trouble holding a constant altitude in a turn. His ridicule got to me. I released the flight controls and looked at him sitting next to me in the T-37 cockpit. I said something to the effect that I knew I could fly and had done extremely well in the introduction program and that any issues now were due to his poor instruction. Furthermore, I told him that I wanted to go back, land, and get another instructor. He laughed and replied it was finally time for me to demonstrate some manliness.

While we didn't immediately return from that flight, a later check ride was effective in getting me a new instructor. I flew the check with the squadron operations officer (he was a good friend with my instructor), didn't do well, and busted the first check ride. I repeated the ride with another check pilot, did well and passed. I also moved from his table to another instructor who had been an F-100 pilot and looked at things much more openly and was operationally oriented.

Because of the failure, I could no longer take a check ride with instructors in my section but had to go to the more experienced check pilots in the Standardization/Evaluation Section. They were honest, very good pilots. Flying with them allowed me to be evaluated against the requirements of the syllabus, not the personality of the instructor. The result was that I quickly rose in the flying order of merit.

Academics during pilot training were very challenging. We studied aerodynamics, physiology, weather, normal and emergency flying procedures, and Morse Code. I did well in most of the classes. However, I was having trouble learning the dits and dahs of Morse Code. B.J. became my mentor and instructor. She would tap a pencil against the dining room table or speak the dots and dashes and I would have to tell her what letter she was transmitting. She learned the Code much faster than me. Her drilling me dramatically improved my ability to recognize and identify the Morse code on the radio and I passed the test.

B.J. also helped me study. Many of the Emergency Procedures had to be committed to memory and flawlessly performed in the airplane, in the simulator, and in the classroom. Her patience in specifying an emergency and requiring me to perfectly quote the procedure was instrumental in my success. At a Silver Wings Orientation Day for wives of student pilots, they had the opportunity to fly in the T-37 simulator. She was doing very well so the instructor activated the Fire Warning light. She immediately executed the emergency procedure, pulled the Fire Tee Handle and shut down the engine. He was very, very impressed.

Another lesson for her at the orientation was about the physiology of flight under high altitude and high-G situations. The instructors explained the effects on the pilot's body and encouraged the wives to feed us a good breakfast to help us avoid potentially debilitating issues in flight. She came home that night to tell me that from now on she was fixing breakfast. I told her that I didn't need breakfast and that it was fine for her to stay in bed. Not to be dissuaded the next morning, she arose with me at 4:30am to fix breakfast before my early report to the flight line. I showered and dressed in flight suit and boots and walked into the kitchen where she had just broken an egg over the burner without putting the frying pan on it. Still too sleepy to see well, she poured the orange juice, missing the glass, but hitting her arm. I put my arms around her and escorted her back to bed saying that I really appreciated the effort, but it wasn't necessary. It may have been one of her happiest moments of our marriage and forever established the course for breakfast (or lack thereof) at our house.

B.J. also did a myriad of other things that put me just a little ahead of pilot training classmates. She regularly polished shoes and boots, ironed uniforms and performed many tasks that I should have done. Occasionally she would go to the base movie theater and see our classmates and their wives who asked about me. She would explain that I was home studying. The result of the teamwork between B.J. and me was that my grades, flying and attitude soared, and I was always in the top 2 or 3 in the class.

Our assignments after graduation were selected based on our class order of merit. We had 42 airplanes and bases that we could place in our desired order. After consulting with B.J., I picked RF-4Cs to Europe as first on list. Based on my rank in pilot training I was selected as a Distinguished Graduate and was assigned to my first choice of RF-4Cs to Toul Rosier, France. We were excited about graduating and moving onward to the "Real Air Force."

For thirteen months we were looking toward Graduation Day as a special day. We had made great friends and would be heading in very different directions. B.J. wanted to look nice at the ceremony. In those days people dressed up for special events. She bought a beautiful dress but didn't have the money to immediately pay for the very feminine white, straw beret hat she loved. After all, it was $12.00. She put down $5.00 and placed it on lay-a-way agreeing to pay a couple of dollars a week until the balance was paid. She finished the payments a few days before graduation and she had her dress, hat and gloves all set.

Mom and Dad drove down from Indiana for the ceremony. After the obligatory speeches and congratulations, Mom and B.J. pinned the new wings on my chest. We were very happy and proud.

While B.J. and my parents stayed at the Reception at the Officers' Club, several of my classmates and I went to an academic room and took the FAA Commercial Pilot's Examination. The tests were graded as soon as we submitted them. I passed and was awarded the Single and Multi-Engine Commercial Pilot License with Instrument Rating. I have continued to use that license for more than a half century of owning and flying civilian airplanes.

The Craig Aero Club had a Cessna 150 and I persuaded John Shiner, the Top Graduate of our pilot training class and a civilian flight instructor, to give me a checkout. After an hour of flying, he signed me off to fly solo. I called B.J. and she came to the flight line. After some smooth talk, she agreed to go flying with me, but had to carry our toy poodle with her. This was only the second time that I had flown an airplane with a propeller, and I took my sweet wife and little dog for a ride. Of course, an Alabama thunderstorm approached as we were landing. After fighting the growing crosswind, I landed and taxied to a stop. She, the dog, and I breathed a sigh of relief. She has been flying with me ever since.

Chapter 6: Moving from Student Pilot to the "Real Air Force"

More Training

As with most academic and training programs, there are many artificialities in pilot training. The Air Training Command was a school house and now we were about to move on to the Tactical Air Command of fighters and a real-world mission.

Before we could begin training in the RF-4C Phantom II, we had to go to Survival School at Stead Air Force Base in Reno, Nevada. B.J. and I drove from Selma, Alabama to her parent's home in Colorado Springs where she stayed for the two weeks I was in Nevada. Arriving at Stead, I was joined by several of my Academy and pilot training classmates along with many other officers and NCOs. We were organized into elements of a dozen or so guys and bused to the Sierra Nevada Mountains. Once there, we had to use parachute canopies to build shelters in the base camp. We learned survival skills and ground map navigation. We tried to remember which plants were safe to eat and which to avoid. A small creek ran through the back of the camp. We were able to catch several crawfish to throw in with our dandelion and carrot soup. After a couple of days, we were given some survival food and taken in teams of twos to a drop off point, assigned a set of destination coordinates and left in the wild. We were told that there were people out there trying to capture us and we were to evade them for the next 24 hours. My teammate for this exercise was an Academy classmate and we headed off with great confidence.

After a night pretending we were Daniel Boone rummaging around mountains and ravines, we began our trek toward our assigned pick-up point. In a couple of hours, we were captured by the "Bad Guys" and taken to a prison camp. For the next two days and a night we were interrogated and isolated. When we only provided Name, Rank and Serial Number we were shoved into a box in which there was only enough room to squat as they slammed the door behind us. It was a very intense time, but we knew it was for only a few hours. I cannot imagine the hardship that the Vietnam Prisoners of War endured without any hint of when they would be free. Many Academy classmates, including my dear friend Leroy Stutz, would spend over six years as Prisoners of War in Vietnam.

At the end of the training we were back at Stead with free time to go into Reno. We also had a coupon for a free dinner at Harrah's Casino. It was good to be back in civilization.

Rejoining B.J. in Colorado Springs, we began our move to Shaw Air Force Base in Sumter, South Carolina. I thought it would be a great idea to stop at the McDonnell Aircraft plant in St. Louis to see them make the airplanes that I would soon be flying. They were very kind to give both of us a tour that was very educational and piqued our excitement of soon strapping one of these beautiful airplanes on my back.

We were again blessed with dear friends who had preceded us to Shaw. Leroy Stutz had been an Academy classmate and he and his wife, Karen, were in our pilot training class. We had become close friends. We called them, and they told us that several of the students were renting trailers. They graciously agreed to find one for us. Thanks to them, we had a place to immediately drop our bags when we arrived. It was a two-bedroom, one bath trailer home located on some farm property. While certainly not equal to our house on Craig Air Force Base, it was more than adequate.

The trailer park was owned by a man and wife who had six or eight kids of the his, hers, and theirs relationship. Since this was before double-wide trailers, they had put two trailers together with a connecting walkway. We went back to Graysville at Christmas and returned to a mess in the trailer park. In their desire to improve their little trailer park, they had helped someone clean out a chicken house, then decided that the chicken droppings would be great fertilizer for the lawns in the trailer park. Unfortunately, it had rained the night before we returned. The stench and mess were immediately obvious while we were still in the car. I quickly went to the owner's trailer and demanded that he provide some kind of a walkway to our trailer. Almost immediately, kids began pouring out of the two trailers with lumber in hand to lay down a sidewalk from our parking spot to the front door. We couldn't get rid of the smell or the mess, but we could function despite it. Our little toy poodle, Angel, wasn't happy about having to squat in it. I often wondered if the yard was plush after all the "fertilizer" dissolved into the soil. We were only there for three months and didn't see a need to go back years later to see the results.

The RF-4C's extended nose housed low and high-altitude cameras.

At the RF-4C school I was crewed with Dick Applehans, a bachelor and instructor at Craig AFB when I was going through pilot training. We had met there once, but I was disappointed that I would be crewed with him. I was hoping that I would have a married pilot so that B.J. and his wife could communicate when we were flying or deployed. Dick and I did all the academic and flying training together and we did well. We completed our simulator and flight checks and were declared ready to go to our next assignment in France. We finished the training in December 1965 and were given the option to remain in the U.S. to enjoy Christmas and get our family settled before we were to report in France in early January 1966.

Off to France (1966)

Because there was a lack of on-base housing, B.J. could not accompany me to France until I found off-base living quarters that met USAF standards. Again, B.J. moved into her parent's house in Colorado Springs. She would stay there until I found a house and completed the paper-work that authorized her to move to join me. With her safely and comfortably set in Colorado, I went to Toul Rosier Air Base, located about 25 miles from Nancy, France, in the region that had been battlefields in many past wars, including both WWI and WWII.

Upon arrival I wanted to quickly go through the process to find a place to live so that I could send for B.J. I was introduced to a French-speaking USAF sergeant who would be pleased to escort me in finding a house or apartment. There weren't very many apartments available near the base. We finally found a one-bedroom apartment on Rue de Liberacion in Nancy. The street was named after the famed march by General Patton into the center of Nancy where he would establish his WWII headquarters in the final push into Germany.

Before B.J. could come, she had to have the necessary immunizations. Since she had no inoculations as a child, she had to have the entire battery. Finally, with the apartment rented and B.J. finished with shots, I completed the paper work for her to come to France. She and our dog arrived in Paris early on Easter Sunday Morning, 1966. We had a great second honeymoon visiting the tourist sights, enjoying the food, and reacquainting ourselves with each other. Too soon we had to head back to Nancy and the reality of me working 25 miles from her with only one car.

The apartment was on the second floor with a small balcony off the living room that projected out toward the main street. That street led to Place Stanislas, a beautiful garden in Nancy with gold encrusted gates, gorgeous flowers, and flowing pathways. Our street also was the main passage way from the university to areas where students lived. Upon occasion, B.J. would be on the balcony looking for me to come home. The students would stop under her balcony and recite *Romeo and Juliet* to her in French.

Another unique aspect of our little apartment was that it had no telephone. Of course, this was long before cell phones. Consequently, if there was an exercise the base had to call the patisserie across the street. The owners lived above the store and agreed that we could use their phone. They spoke little English and we less French. But it worked out. Moreover, B.J. used the excuse to visit them to get to know them and learn more French in their patisserie. In the process she began to love their pastry delicacies and would bring them home. Consequently, we quickly gained weight from over indulging.

As new guys in the squadron, Dick and I began our training under the watchful eye of leadership and instructors. After a dozen or so training flights, we were administered our final check ride during a deployment to Moron Air Base, Seville, Spain. Now declared fully Combat Ready, we returned home to put the finishing touches on our skills.

After about three months, B.J. and I were offered on-base housing and we moved into a very nice single-family home. We quickly unpacked from our move from the apartment in Nancy and I went back to flying nearly every day.

We were able to take a couple of trips while we were in France. B.J. went with a group of ladies to the Keukenhof Gardens in The Netherlands. She was immediately impressed with size and beauty of the Gardens and the countryside and added a return trip to her "Bucket List." Another trip was to Southern Germany and Switzerland. Our lack of language proficiency produced some funny results.

Gil and his wife, Pam, our good friends from the Academy and a fellow pilot from our squadron, invited us for a picnic. We stopped at a little store to buy some bread, cheese and wine. The owner was being especially nice. My German was of no value and Gil's French wasn't much better. The owner explained that there was a little red ball in the

85

cap of the wine. Then he made gestures pointing toward the bottle and we nodded. When we opened the wine, the wives, Gil and I surmised that the little red ball was to put in the wine to make it effervesce. We dropped it in the wine and expectantly watched it drift to the bottom. Nothing! Oh well. Several days later we were in the Officer's Club and asked the bartender. He showed us a small plastic box and explained that if we saved 24 of the plastic balls, we could exchange the box and balls for another bottle of cheap wine. He said he liked that wine when he went fishing. So much for our time trying to be sophisticated.

Our last trip was from France to Southern Germany and Austria. We stopped at several places along the way to tour castles and historical sites. The most memorable stop was along a country road in Austria. We saw a rolling meadow that looked like the one Julie Andrews ran up the hill singing, *"The Sound of Music."* We couldn't resist. B.J. climbed over the fence, went to the bottom of the hill, turned, and ran up the hill recreating the iconic scene. I thought she sounded better than Julie Andrews. But the cows just looked at her as if to say, "Another crazy American trying to be Julie Andrews."

However, our joy of being in Europe was about to be truncated. In 1966 President de Gaulle was on a crusade to get out from under U.S. military dominance. He was not happy that the U.S. retained the launch codes and keys to nuclear weapons. He wanted to control his weapons and didn't want the U.S. involved. It seems that he quickly forgot that only a couple of decades earlier, it was the U.S. that liberated his country from the Germans and had we not become involved he would be speaking German. Regardless, tensions were escalating for the U.S. military to leave France.

Many of the French people picked up on his anger and began treating Americans with disrespect and near hatred. They were a proud people, especially of the French language. If we didn't speak French, often they would not speak English even though most were fluent or at least conversant in it.

Chapter 7: Spotlight 088: From France to Vietnam

Spotlight 088 Was Classified, But Everyone Could Guess

We had been in France less than eight months when I found that the flight scheduling board had been completely wiped clean. When I questioned the sudden change, I was told to quietly go into the briefing room, sit down, and shut up. Very soon the Wing Commander arrived with a classified telegram ordering Project Spotlight 088. Our squadron of pilots, navigators, crew chiefs, support personnel and airplanes would be re-designated to the 32nd TRS and immediately deployed to Southeast Asia. We would be based at Tan Son Nhut Air Base, near Saigon, Vietnam. Fortunately, the Air Force arranged for our airplanes to be flown by other F-4C crews from France to Mountain Home AFB, Idaho. The substitute aircrews allowed us to accompany our families back to the States. We were told to go home, inform our families, decide where they would go, and report back to the personnel office at 1:00pm.

B.J. and I quickly decided that she would go back to Colorado Springs until I returned from Vietnam. Since we had recently moved and didn't have much furniture to ship, we decided to pack the next day and depart for home the following day. I went to the personnel office and found the lengthy line snaking through a dormitory. At the first door, I told them that B.J. would go to Colorado Springs and we could be packed the next day. As we progressed through the line, we received the shots required for Vietnam, completed short form wills, reviewed our personnel records for completeness, and finished other administrative details. All of this was necessary since we were deploying to a combat area. The completed forms and details would be required for this move and, heaven forbid, if we were shot down. By the end of the line, we had written orders in hand, the time that the movers would arrive, and the orders to ship our VW bug to the U.S.

Our first snag was when we learned that there was an airline strike in the United States and reservations could not be made. It would be our responsibility to ship our pets home. B.J. and a neighbor loaded Angel in the car, drove her to Luxembourg and arranged flights for the dog to Colorado Springs. There was no mention of a pet embargo. B.J. arrived back home as the packers were leaving with our worldly possessions. We spent the night in the Visiting Officers' Quarters.

The next morning, we loaded on the bus to Frankfurt Air Base, Germany for our flight back home. Arriving the next day in New York, the reality of the airline strike immediately became apparent. Flights out of New York were overbooked. Moreover, we learned that our dog had gone from Luxembourg to Brussels to London, only to be turned back to Brussels because there was an embargo on live animals into the U.S. due to the strike. B.J. used her experience with Braniff to talk the counter manager into sending a wire stating that Braniff would accept our dog and guarantee its further shipment to Colorado Springs. I saw a box behind the counter with a squadron mate's name on it and asked the manager to ship it to Denver. He agreed, and those cats continued on their way.

The Air Force did a fantastic job for us. They expedited our departure from France and marked our orders with a classified note that gave us priority on the airlines during the strike. Spotlight 088 became our code for getting on board flights and making hotel arrangements. Finally, we were on a flight to Chicago, then to Terre Haute for a couple of days with my parents in Graysville.

We checked with B.J.'s dad and found that our dog, Angel, had not arrived. A few calls later we found where she was being held and arranged for the trip to the Springs. The airline people nearly killed her with kindness. We had left enough food for several days in the kennel, but they gave it to her all at once. She, like we, didn't have much discipline about controlling her appetite and ate the whole portion. Her stomach expanded and some of her intestines were ruptured, but she made it to Colorado Springs. A few vet visits and dollars later, she fully recovered.

After a couple of days, we left Graysville retracing the same flights I had taken some half dozen years before in my trek from the farm to The Academy. B.J. settled with her parents in a small bedroom in their home. We arranged for me to continue to Idaho to connect with our USAF airplanes for the final leg to Vietnam.

There was an added complication. My bag with all my flight gear including parachute harness, helmet, flight suits and other equipment that I would need to fly in Vietnam was lost between Graysville and Colorado Springs. I was required to go to Mt. Home AFB a day early to get new equipment for the deployment. Interestingly, many months later the bag mysteriously arrived at my squadron building in Saigon. All the equipment, including my personal weapon, was still in the bag. I returned the government equipment and flew with my little automatic pistol in my flight suit.

We spent our last night together in a motel near Stapleton Airport in Denver. It was less than two weeks from our orders to leave France until I was leaving the U.S. for Vietnam. I had an early morning flight and B.J. took me to the airport. I will never forget being on the plane, pushing back from the airport in the pre-dawn darkness, and looking up into the terminal where the silhouette of young woman stood alone, peering at my airplane, watching her husband off to war, wondering if he would return home to her. Nine months later I did come home, and she did meet me at the same airport.

B.J. worked in Colorado Springs at a travel agency using the skills she had learned at Braniff. She found a nice apartment in the northern part of town. There were several other military wives living in the complex there while their husbands were in Vietnam. When the furniture arrived, it had been nearly destroyed in transit from France. The train carrying the large wooden boxes of household goods had a wreck and our box tumbled several times. When the box finally arrived and was opened, B.J. sat down and cried. There were holes punched in the sofa.

Many dishes and glasses were broken. She called her dad and together they pieced together enough furniture and household goods to last until I returned. She fought through all the paper work to file a claim for reimbursement of our damages. In some ways, destroying our household goods was a blessing – they were from Railroad Salvage in Selma and not very good. We used the monetary settlement to buy nicer furniture when we arrived in Germany.

We had shipped our little VW bug from France to the Port of Chicago. My dad and a friend picked it up and drove it to Abilene, Kansas where B.J. had flown to meet him. She drove it back to Colorado and it served her well in my absence and in the snow.

Sometimes she would not get a letter or hear from me for a week. Once it was over two weeks. She came home from work and there was an official USAF car in the parking lot near where she usually parked. Those cars only came to the apartment area with bad news. She stopped, put her head on the steering wheel and prayed. While it was terrible news for someone in the apartment complex, it was not for her. Those kinds of events and news of the war were always more meaningful since she was now personally affected by the activities occurring a half-world away.

Vietnam Tour (1966-1967)

In Vietnam I was assigned to a flight commanded by Lew Andrews, a West Point graduate, Christian, and very good pilot. Lew was an effective mentor and leader. His wife, Betts, and their children lived in Colorado Springs while we were in Vietnam. Betts became a faithful friend and surrogate mom to B.J. while Lew and I were in Vietnam. They talked often and updated each other with the latest news from either of us.

I was stationed Tan Son Nhut Air Base near Saigon, Vietnam. I continued to be crewed with Dick Applehans and flew with other pilots and instructors as the need arose. Early in the war there was a policy that the length of tour could be reduced by one month for every 20 missions flown in North Vietnam. I flew more than 60 missions in the North before that policy was terminated. Consequently, I was able to reduce my tour from twelve to nine months. I flew another 15 or so missions in North Vietnam and about 125 missions in South Vietnam and Laos for a total of 202 missions.

One feature of the RF-4C was the High Frequency radio. We could channel it to the ham radio bands, contact one of the operators in the U.S., and they would give us a phone patch to our wives. The infrequent calls permitted a closer connection than the letters. It was always better to hear B.J.'s voice than read her letters. When one side was finished talking, they had to say "Over" so that the ham operator could switch his radios from send to receive. The ending phrase between husband and wife became, "*I love you, over.*"

The RF-4C Phantom II was derived from the F-4H originally operated by the Navy. The Air Force redesigned portions and called it the F-4C. The airplane that I flew was further modified to the RF version with an extended nose area housing several still cameras and an infrared sensor. A side looking radar was installed in the former missile bays along each side of the nose. It carried no armament except for the .38 Special revolvers in the vests of the pilots. Consequently, our mission was to find the enemy, precisely locate them, and return with film to be processed and analyzed at our home base. Intelligence gained from these missions was then sent to a combat center that organized armed strikes against the targets.

Each squadron has a distinctive patch worn on their flight suits. Our patch was a continuation of a WWII reconnaissance squadron of a crow with a camera. Above it was embroidered, "*Alone! Unarmed! Unafraid?*". We seldom flew in formation and were "*Alone!*" on the missions. We certainly were "*Unarmed!*" The question mark following the "*Unafraid?*" was appropriate. Some missions, especially those over South Vietnam, were minimal risk and the fear was quite low.

"Alone! Unarmed! Unafraid?" 12th TRS patch

However, our missions over North Vietnam, especially at night, were increased risk. I was blessed to fly out of Saigon early in the war and before the surface to air missiles (SAMs) moved south of the Hanoi area. We did not have the range to reach Hanoi. Aircraft based in Thailand performed those very dangerous missions.

Our missions into North Vietnam generally went to the passes from North Vietnam into Laos through which the supplies for the North Vietnam Army (NVA) were transported, usually at night to avoid being attacked by our fighters and bombers. The lifeline to the NVA became famously known as the Ho Chi Minh Trail. They made great attempts to disguise it, cover it, use it at night or move it. Our mission was to find the trail and the truck stops along the way.

The most challenging of the missions was to Mu Gia Pass at night. It ran in a NE/SW orientation and was several miles long. The only way to attack and overfly the full length was from one end to the other. The mountains prevented any other approach and there was no way to vary our attack path. To get good intelligence, we had to be no higher than 1000 feet above the trails that were in the deepest part of the pass. At that altitude we were well below the tops of the karst mountains through which the trails ran.

The RF-4C was equipped with terrain following radar that looked ahead and could give us a picture of any mountains in front of us. It also gave us climb and dive indications on the flight director. We used the TFR to descend into the target area, then work down to the desired altitude below the ridges and to guide us through the pass. To trigger the cameras and light the ground, we carried photo-flash cartridges that were ejected from the RF-4C and exploded behind us with sufficient brilliance that the cameras could photograph anything below us. Obviously, we woke up any sleeping troops and they quickly manned their guns. Fortunately, the cartridges exploded well behind us and we were accelerating away from them. Anti-aircraft guns engaged us on every mission to the passes. However, the gunners apparently had never been bird hunters. Had they been, they would have known to shoot in front of the airplane rather than shoot where we had been. With thankfulness to God, I was never hit.

Most of our missions in South Vietnam were at night using our infrared sensor searching for enemy encampments. We had no readouts in the cockpit. The film had to be returned to the base, processed, and interpreted. When an encampment or concentration of enemy forces or supplies was found, that information was quickly forwarded to those responsible for assigning combat forces to take them out. Ground forces, artillery, fighters or even B-52s could be used, depending on the location and size of the enemy. Periodically we were told that we found a hidden company of soldiers or a truck stop, and that fighters and bombers were dispatched to destroy them before they could inflict damage on American and Allied troops.

Normally, we extinguished all the airplane's lights at night. We would periodically turn them on to get the gunners to fire small arms at us thus revealing their positions. We could then call in fighters that were on alert to attack them. On a mission just north of the DMZ we found the construction of a missile site and called in the alert fighters which destroyed it before it was operational and could engage our aircraft. This was the first SA-2 missile site that far south and it was not rebuilt by the time I left Vietnam. For this mission and the combined efforts of the over 200 missions I flew, I was awarded the Distinguished Flying Cross and fourteen Air Medals.

It was a great tragedy that many warriors did not come home from Vietnam and for many who did come home, Vietnam never left them. While I was in Vietnam, we lost one aircraft and two crewmembers on a night mission. There were not found, and it is assumed that they hit a mountain. After I left, my aircraft commander, Dick Applehans decided to stay for another six months. He never returned from a night mission which was similar to the ones that he and I had flown many times. His back-seater was later found deceased.

Our dear friend Leroy Stutz, an Academy and pilot training classmate, who, with his wife Karen, had arranged for our trailer in Sumter, South Carolina, was shot down and taken captive. He was held in various prison camps, including the Hanoi Hilton, in North Vietnam for six and one-half years. His torture, like for all of them, was inhumane and tragic. While he did return home, he still has physical pain and issues from the multiple beatings by the North Vietnamese.

When Karen learned of his shoot down and potential capture, she called B.J. who immediately jumped on an airliner and went to her side. It was a couple of years before the North Vietnamese admitted that they had captured Leroy. Karen and their son visited us in Maryland while Leroy was a POW. One of the core principles of military service is taking care of each other. Interestingly, Leroy and Karen returned to Hanoi about thirty years after his release. He was permitted to visit the Hanoi Hilton and see his old cell. Time is a great healer on both sides of war.

Karl Richter was another Academy and pilot training classmate. He and I alternated being number 2 or number 3 in our pilot training class. He was a bachelor and often came to our house for a home-cooked meal. He and his Dodge Hemi were a legend at our base. Karl often participated in drag racing on the weekend. Occasionally he tried it on base and earned a few days of suspension from driving his car.

Karl flew F-105s out of Thailand into the most heavily defended areas of North Vietnam. He refused to come home after his 100 missions and volunteered for another 100. He had shot down a North Vietnamese MIG fighter aircraft and was known to always get his target. I happened to see him at the Tan Son Nhut Officers' Club. He was in Saigon to receive an award from the South Vietnamese Government and it was presented to him by its president. Karl was spending the night at our base before going back to Thailand. He and I had dinner and spent the evening discussing the war and the political failures that led to it and wouldn't finish it. I asked him why he was extending to fly more of the most dangerous missions that were in the war. He quickly replied that since he was a bachelor, he would remain so that we husbands could go home to our families.

A month or so after the dinner with Karl, I went home to B.J. and to our new assignment at Ramstein, Germany. Within a day or two of arriving in Germany I learned that Karl had been shot down and successfully ejected but died when his parachute hit one of the huge karst pinnacles that were in the mountains between North Vietnam and Laos. They were able to recover his body. Because of Karl's dedication and performance in combat, he became an icon at the Air Force Academy. Our class commissioned a statue of him that is prominently displayed to all incoming freshmen as well as the entire cadet wing. He is an exemplar of the true meaning of Duty, Honor, Country.

I have highest respect for all who served in Vietnam. Our country did not support us, our president didn't support us, and our families were often harassed because of us. Our squadron flew difficult and dangerous missions. However, they were not close to the same danger as those into the far northern areas of Vietnam and Hanoi and Haiphong. Each mission into what was known as Route Pack 6 was sure to be met with MIGs, SAMs and intense ground fire.

In fact, we had it relatively easy in Saigon. Most of our squadron aircrews were bedded down in an old French Estate in the outskirts of Saigon. We also employed the previous Vietnamese caretaker couple who cooked great meals and helped with translations. Lew Andrews took about 12 of us to live in an old hotel about a half mile down the street from the others. We could walk or use a squadron truck to get back and forth to the base or the other area for meals. We could also take taxis to downtown Saigon to enjoy a dinner out in a nice Vietnamese or French restaurant.

The Air Force arranged for us to have some Rest and Relaxation time. About every three months we could submit a request for a week of R&R in Bangkok, Tokyo, or Hong Kong. I used those trips to buy little things for B.J. I bought her a beaded suit and a dress in Hong Kong and jewelry in Bangkok. In Bangkok I bought a star black sapphire stone for my Academy ring.

The biggest and best R&R was to meet B.J. in Honolulu. She was working in a travel agency and made reservations for us at the Ilikai Hotel on Waikiki Beach. The night before I was to leave Saigon for

Hawaii one of our guys got sick and I was asked to take his mission. I quickly agreed but soon began having second thoughts. The mission was into North Vietnam and would not land until after B.J. had left Colorado Springs. I wasn't as concerned about getting shot down, because I knew they would do everything possible to recover us. I was concerned that if I was shot down, I wouldn't get back in time to make the plane to meet her. We did get shot at, but not hit, and I landed in time to return to my room, shower and pack before I had to make the plane to Hawaii.

She flew to Hawaii and shared a room with another wife who was meeting her husband, then met me at the terminal when I landed. We could hardly recognize each other. We each had lost lots of weight and were much thinner than when we had said goodbye at the Denver Airport about six months earlier.

In addition to the joy of being together, enjoying the Hawaiian lifestyle, and beach, there was another event that shaped our lives. As we were lying on the beach, we saw an older lady pushing her husband in a wheelchair. She was having trouble pushing him in the sand. We walked over to help her. She explained that they had been farmers in the Midwest and had saved their money for a dream trip to Hawaii. As his health began to fail, they decided now was the time they would take the trip together.

As we walked back to our spot on the beach, we marveled at their dedication to both save and then to make the trip. We agreed that we would do those kinds of trips when we were young and healthy. That commitment has meant that we spent our money early and didn't save as we should have. However, we and our kids have travelled the world, skiing, scuba diving, and otherwise enjoying God's creation. We don't regret making the decision to seize the moment and enjoy life with each other, our kids, and our grandkids.

Brother Bill Watson and Cousin Bud Watson in Vietnam

Both my brother Bill and cousin Bud were drafted into the Army in 1965 and both served in Vietnam during the time I was there. Bill was in Army training when I was going through RF-4C training. B.J. and I rented an airplane and flew to see him at Fort Jackson where he was receiving his initial training. I would see him several months later on the other side of the world.

I arrived in Vietnam first. Mom sent me a note with the name of the troop transport ship that Bill was on going into Vietnam. I checked the classified records and learned the date he would be in the port at Cam Rahn Bay. I caught a hop to the air force base, and a tender to his ship to surprise him. Arriving at the ship in my flight suit was an experience. They couldn't understand how I learned they were there. Moreover, they weren't happy that I was packing a .38 revolver. I did explain there was a war going on, so they let me keep it. They didn't want to call him, but I persuaded them that I was a legitimate brother and he was called. We visited for a bit, then got permission to go on shore together. I was concerned that my unscheduled arrival to the ship and insistence on seeing him would cause problems for him. However, his superiors apparently thought more about it and let it pass. Bill's tour was with the Army Combat Engineers and was spent building facilities at Cam Rahn Bay, Phan Rang and nearby locations. During our mutual tours, he came to Saigon a couple of times and we both went to the Bob Hope 1966 Christmas Show.

Bill and I Enjoying Dinner in Saigon 1966
A long way from the farm in Indiana

Bud's Vietnam tour began with being stationed Northwest of Saigon in Tay Ninh Province. A couple of times he volunteered to ride security on resupply convoys that came to the Port of Saigon. He could get a pass to visit me at the air base. When he came, he stayed in one of the rooms in our squadron housing and I would take him into downtown Saigon for dinner. Toward the end of his tour he was relocated to the northern part of South Vietnam. Unfortunately, he was often on very dangerous long-range reconnaissance missions into areas that were extensively defoliated with Agent Orange. He died too soon after returning home from complications resulting from that chemical.

Chapter 8: Back to B.J. and Returning to Europe and Normalcy

Ramstein Air Base, Germany (1967-1970)

Upon completing the tour in Vietnam, I was assigned to the 38th Tactical Reconnaissance Squadron (TRS) located at Ramstein AB, Germany. Returning to the U.S., B.J. met me at the same Denver Airport that I had left on the way to Vietnam. We packed up our few belongings in Colorado Springs, sold our VW Bug, and began heading for our third foreign assignment in a year. After visiting her family, we had a few days in Indiana before catching flights to Frankfurt, Germany. Unlike going to France, on base housing was available and B.J. and I could travel together to our new assignment. We flew into Frankfurt and took Air Force transportation to Ramstein, about three-hours away. After checking into the base guest quarters, we walked over to the Officers' Club for dinner. As we walked into the bar area, there were several couples from our squadrons in France and Vietnam who immediately let out a cheer and welcomed us. We were home.

In checking on housing, I was greeted by the sergeant that had helped me find an apartment in France. When he left Toul Rosier, he was reassigned to Ramstein. After exchanging pleasantries, he took me aside to tell that me he had learned I was enroute to Ramstein and had reserved an apartment for me. I said I wanted to look at it. He told me it was on the first floor of a four-story walk-up apartment building and if I didn't take it right then, a more senior officer would grab it. I signed without inspecting it. Thanks to him, I may have been the only First Lieutenant that had a first-floor apartment. It is always good to treat people well wherever and whenever you meet them. You may meet them again.

38th Tactical Reconnaissance Squadron.

Since I had checked out as an Aircraft Commander in Vietnam, I was immediately assigned to that role and introduced to Major Lino DeMichieli who would be my back seater. Lino was a few years older and was fully qualified in the RF-4C. We were a good team in the air and on the ground. Lino had grown up in Indianapolis, Indiana as the older son of Italians who had immigrated into the U.S. soon after WWI. We were blessed to learn that he and Andrea lived in the same building we had just been assigned, but on the fourth floor of another stairwell. B.J. and Andrea became dear friends and we have stayed close since our tour there.

Our squadron was a perfect harmony of experienced pilots and navigators integrated with us young guns fresh from combat tours in Vietnam. This mixture of experience and enthusiasm blended to create highly qualified aircrews. The older guys took us younger ones under their wings and taught us the intricacies of reconnaissance flying low level in an environment that was training for the potential of a large ground war with Russia which was anticipated to be launched from East Germany into West Germany.

Flying in Germany in the 1960s was fantastic with very few rules about low altitude and high airspeed. However, winter weather brought low ceilings and visibilities that limited our ability to train. It was back to Spain as we had done from France.

Flying with Lino was especially rewarding when we deployed to Italy for additional training. He was fluent in Italian. Moreover, he could very quickly pick up local dialect. When we were on an Italian Air Base, he did all the talking and we were extremely well received. As a going away present to our hosts at a hotel on Rimini Beach, we overflew the hotel early on a Sunday morning taking the pictures with our reconnaissance camera. We had the pictures printed, framed and mailed to the hotel management. They loved the picture and posted it in a prominent place in their lobby. However, they did say that their guests didn't want any more low altitude flybys at 8:00 on Sunday morning.

Our First Son Is Born (May 13, 1968)

The first time that B.J. went to the hair stylist in a small town near our base, the lady asked her if she had any children. She replied no. The lady then told her she would leave Germany with a baby and a Cuckoo Clock. She was right.

In the Fall soon after we arrived in Germany, we took a long weekend to go to the famous Oktoberfest in Munich and followed the opening parade into the Hofbrau Tent. B.J. couldn't understand why she was having to go to the bathroom so often. Soon after we returned home, she learned the reason – she was pregnant.

The pregnancy went well. Andrea, Sindy Schwab and other friends hosted a wonderful baby shower. Both sets of our parents sent the necessary baby supplies from home and we purchased many nice things in Germany. We found a baby crib in base housing supply and bought a rocker. A little paint on both, some Winnie The Pooh curtains and decorations, and we were set for Derek's arrival.

One of the challenges during her pregnancy was my frequent flying, including spending a couple weeks at a time in Spain. There was one advantage to going to Spain. The oranges were wonderful and a case of them fit nicely around the cameras in the nose of the RF-4C. B.J. became addicted to fresh oranges, as did Derek. He still loves fresh orange juice.

I was selected to be on the team that represented the United States in a NATO reconnaissance competition named Royal Flush. It was a night competition to find and photograph specific sites in Germany and nearby countries. We practiced nearly every night for about six months. On one flight completing a low approach at our base to get under the clouds to go to the next target, we were struck by lightning. The bolt hit on top of the radome about six feet in front of my face. I was immediately blinded. I had my back seater read me the instruments and made a slight climb while turning on the very bright storm lights. My vision began returning and we flew until I could see well enough to land. It was about midnight and the thunder from the lightning strike was so loud that it woke B.J. (about 7 months pregnant) and she jumped straight up in bed. I got home a few hours later and together we thanked God for His protection. When the airplane was inspected severe damage was found. The radome had cracked and cut the pitot static lines taking out the airspeed, altitude, and other indicators. The camera section had thick glass windows which were shattered resulting in shards of glass going through both engines. The honeycomb on the stabilizer was separated where the lightning energy departed the airplane. Our fantastically talented maintenance professionals had it back flying in about a week.

It seems that big events occur in multiples. I continued to get ready for Royal Flush and Derek continued to grow. B.J.'s parents came to Germany for his long-anticipated birth. When they arrived, I went to the cleaners to get my competition flight suit. While I was there, B.J.'s water broke. I returned home to find that Lino and Andrea were rushing her to the hospital. I took a short cut and arrived at the same time they did. Both Lino and I were in flight suits. The first question from the admitting nurse was, "Which of you is the dad?" Several hours later, B.J. delivered a healthy bouncing boy and I went home to get ready to fly that night.

Derek Thomas Watson joined our family on May 13, 1968. B.J. and Derek stayed in the hospital a couple of days while I flew in the competition. Since I was flying nearly every night, I visited during the daytime. That caused some in the hospital to wonder if she was married since I wasn't visiting her at night. We brought Derek home to his especially prepared room and we won the competition the next evening.

Most expectant parents pick out their child's name long before birth. Derek received his name a little differently. Early in the pregnancy we attended a NATO function that honored the crews that would participate in Royal Flush. While there we met a British pilot whose name was Derek. That night we talked about Watson being an English name and that Derek Watson sounded good. However, we couldn't decide on a middle name. The doctor who delivered him asked B.J. what his name would be, and she didn't have an answer for his middle name. He demanded that while Derek was a fine name, he also had to have a Christian name. We ran through the various Biblical names finally settling on Thomas. The doctor was pleased with our selection, and we are as well. Derek seems happy too. However, unknown to me, there had been a Watson tradition that the first son of each generation would have Warren somewhere in his name. We failed in that detail. We were very happy that B.J.'s parents were there for the birth, Derek and B.J. came home, and we won the competition. All was going quite well.

The following year we again flew the Royal Flush night competition. As we were attacking the last target, the photoflash cartridge exploded, and I could see we were in the clouds. I shoved the stick forward and told my back-seater to turn the radar to terrain following so that I could see if any hills were in the way. I pulled up before they became a problem. Our competitors did not try to attack the target and couldn't understand how we had been able to get the pictures. I credited my time in Vietnam for the experience to safely go where others feared to tread. Since we got the target and the others didn't, it was a decisive win for our team.

Our tour at Ramstein continued another two years. Derek was baptized by Air Force Chaplain Shoemaker, the same chaplain that had married us at The Academy four years earlier. He was now stationed at Ramstein as were we. Life was good. We often went skiing in Austria with our dear friends, Charles and Sindy Schwab, who became Derek's Godparents. We won another Royal Flush. We bought a Cuckoo Clock but didn't add any more babies while in Germany.

Travel in Europe

. Our off-base time was very enjoyable. While B.J. was pregnant with Derek, we took a trip to Berlin. Since 1968 was at the height of the Cold War and I was a combat pilot with security clearances, we could only travel to Berlin on the "Troop Train." We boarded the train in West Germany and shared a sleeping compartment with our friends. Travelling through East Germany during the night, we were stopped at several check points where the East German and Russian soldiers looked under the train. Based on the post WWII agreements, they were not permitted on board the train. Arriving in West Berlin we went to a pre-arranged hotel and took a couple of tours. The most interesting excursion was into East Berlin through the infamous Berlin Wall and Checkpoint Charlie. Again, we had to be on a military bus and the military members had to wear uniforms. Crossing into East Berlin we had to stop. Those in military uniforms could stay on the bus. But the women not in uniform had to get off the bus, form up in a straight line and have their passports inspected. The East Germans and Russians were allowed on the bus but could only look at our ID cards. Finally, all was well, and we proceeded.

The starkness of the difference between West Berlin and East Berlin was staggering. The Western side was affluent, rebuilt and thriving. People were on the streets and happily proceeding with their activities. East Berlin still showed the damages of WWII. Most buildings had not been rebuilt. Very few stores were open, and they didn't appear to be well stocked. There were very few people on the streets and their faces were downcast. Back to West Berlin we stopped at the Checkpoint Charlie museum and saw many examples of the ways that East Germans had escaped into the West sectors, and the unfortunate results of those who were discovered.

Fifty years later (June 2018) we were in Israel and travelled between the Israeli and Muslim sectors of the West Bank. While the contrast was not as stark as between West and East Berlin, the clear differences reminded us of our trip to Berlin. There were checkpoints in and out of the West Bank sector. The Israeli held territories were clean. The Muslim sectors were not. Even in Jerusalem where the divisions are between neighborhoods, there is a distinction between the two. Clearly, there are social, economic and cultural differences that are manifested in political divisions.

We had other trips throughout Europe. In addition to skiing, we were able to take trips around the countryside. Wine Fest time is very special there. When Derek was only a few months old, we took him and Charles and Sindy in our square back VW down the Mosel and up the Rhine stopping at several villages along the way. Charles spoke perfect German and we had a wonderful time visiting with the local Germans. We took a can of sterno and Derek's formula. When he got hungry, we stopped and heated his bottle. He was a great traveler.

Mom, Dad, Uncle Gay, and Aunt Jeanette came to visit about half-way through our tour. We loaded everyone in two cars and went to Holland, Belgium, all over West Germany, and into Austria. As we turned off the autobahn onto a secondary road into Austria, I noticed that the other car didn't follow. Oh my, no phone, they had no idea where they were, and they spoke no German. We waited a few minutes, then backtracked hoping to find them. At the Autobahn, I turned in the direction we were previously headed and prayed. A few miles later there was a U.S. Military gas station and we pulled off. They were sitting, enjoying a coke, and waiting for us. Rejoined, we continued the trip. During our trip Derek had contracted a very serious upper respiratory cold, complete with runny nose and fever. He couldn't sleep at night. My mom was her normal super grandmother-self and took him into her room where he would sleep in her arms. It was good to get back to Ramstein, but sad to see them leave to go back to Indiana.

As previously mentioned, we won the second Royal Flush. One of the benefits was that we were well known in the USAF and with the manufacturers of our airplanes and reconnaissance equipment. B.J. and I rented an aero club airplane and flew from Germany to the Paris

Air Show. When we arrived at the McDonnell chalet, their representative in Germany recognized me and invited us to join them. Inside, their CEO announced they had won a big contract, grabbed B.J., picked her up and gave her a big hug, then went around the room congratulating everyone. Two executives from Texas Instruments were there and I explained how their infrared sensor helped us in Vietnam and in Royal Flush. They invited us to join them for dinner. They sent a car and we enjoyed the elaborate dinner given as only Texans can. On the way back to the airport, we stopped at a bakery and bought enough French bread to fill the backseat of our little airplane. Once home, we delivered the fresh bread to our friends. Later, Texas Instruments offered me a job and I flew back to Texas for interviews. However, I was led to stay in the Air Force and respectfully declined their offer.

Our time at Ramstein was one of our favorite assignments. The people were fantastic professionals with wonderful families, Germany was affordable then, Derek was born there, and we had a jump start on our Air Force career. We have held a 38th Squadron Reunion every two years for the past couple of decades. We value those reunions as an immense pleasure to rejoin Lino and Andrea, Charles and Sindy, and the other couples that meant so much to us then and continue to be life-long friends now. We held our 2018 reunion in Dayton, Ohio at the USAF Museum and are looking forward to our next reunion in 2020 in Seattle.

Chapter 9: From the Cockpit to the Desk

Returning to the United States and a New Assignment in Maryland (1970-1972)

We packed our belongings that had significantly grown during our three years in Germany. We now had furniture, a cuckoo clock, and Derek, who had also grown. Just as we had left France, we went to Frankfurt and boarded a charter flight home. The flight was not pleasant, it was long, and Derek had diarrhea. Two parents and a screaming child do not fit, nor do they function well, in an airplane lavatory, for even a few minutes let alone seven hours. Both B.J. and I were looking for ejection handles to either extricate ourselves or the other one. I am sure that the people sitting around us were looking for ejection handles for all three of us. In due time we arrived back in the Good Ole USA.

We had purchased a new Ford car from the Base Exchange System and had it delivered to a dealer just outside McGuire AFB, NJ. We went to the dealership and they had our car ready with road maps and filled with gas. They helped us load our bags and we headed to Andrews AFB near Washington, D.C.

Arriving at the base, I signed in and checked with my new bosses who told me to go find a house and take time to visit parents. It was our first time looking for and buying a house. It was hot, and we knew nothing of the D.C. area. But we persisted with our real estate agent and we found a cute house inside the famous Beltway in Oxon Hill, MD.

The house was a nice three-bedroom home with a full basement, much larger than our on-base apartment had been at Ramstein. It was on about an acre of woods with mature trees throughout the neighborhood. The back deck had a view into the woods and the basement walked out into the woods. The commute to Andrews was only about 20 minutes since I was going opposite to those living outside the Beltway but travelling into Washington for work. With the house purchased, it was off to Graysville to see my parents and introduce Derek, now about two-years old, to the rest of the Watson family.

My assignment was to the Air Force Systems Command. Its responsibility was to design, test, and procure equipment for the operational Air Force. I started with the configuration control group that ensured that any modifications to existing or in-design equipment would not interfere with other equipment in the system.

In a few months I was selected to serve in a "Think Tank" with another captain and lieutenant colonel and we shared a secretary. Our office was next door to the two-star general, Deputy Commander for Operations. We were to "think outside the box" for both new weapons systems and improved ways to operate current systems. In addition, we tracked current operations of test programs and test ranges, including the Atlantic and Pacific Missile Test Ranges.

We also prepared the speeches and presentations that were scheduled every month to give the commander and staff an update on operations throughout the command. We reported activities, progress to cost and schedule, and any problems that needed senior leadership involvement. One of the test ranges was being used for an operational exercise with not only the U.S. forces, but NATO units as well. It was a very complex scheduling and utilization problem. We prepared the boss for the briefing the night before and went home late. I came in early to learn that he wasn't totally clear, and I was called into the general's office right before he was to give the briefing to the command leadership. I tried to explain all the colored arrows and the time phasing of the attacks and how our test program would integrate into the flow. Finally, he yelled out to his executive officer, "Bruce, Hal doesn't know what he is talking about either." Another attempt and he understood it as we walked together to the briefing room. He later became a four-star general and commanded this huge command.

One of the departments within this directorate was responsible for the Air Force operations at Edwards AFB, California. Our two-star boss had been the Commander at Edwards prior to this current assignment.

I learned that the division was in the process of selecting the next class of USAF Test Pilots. Based on me working for the boss and knowing the officers on the selection committee, I submitted my application to be a test pilot from which the Space Shuttle crews would be selected. I thought I had a good chance based on my experience, recommendation from the boss, and my reputation with the selection committee.

However, those thoughts were sidetracked the morning that the selection team was leaving for their meeting. My high visibility and success led to being promoted to the rank of Major three years ahead of my year group. It was like a catapult shot toward a successful career. I now had a decision to make: 1) continue to apply for the test pilot school or 2) pursue my plan to fly fighters with the goal of being a tactical wing commander. After calling B.J., we decided to continue to pursue the second option, the plan that we believed God had for us. I walked downstairs to the head of the selection committee and withdrew my application for test pilot school.

A couple of months later, the boss was assigned as the senior USAF officer in Vietnam. When he left, another general replaced him. He was very bright and had been on Secretary McNamara's staff. I soon became his executive officer and spent about 12 hours a day, five or six days a week with him. I learned how to manage the flow of ideas and paper and how to prioritize time. Those demanding and challenging lessons have served well for the rest of my life.

One of the highlights of the job was a one-star general who spent time with me and was a tremendous mentor. He had a PhD and was very astute to how the Air Force works. I stayed in touch with him for a long time after I left that job. He liked B.J. and Derek. If they came to the office, he would push Derek to tell Mom and Dad to get him a Big Mac on the way home. He came to our house about three years later. He played with the boys and reminded them they should have a Big Mac. More about that visit later.

I had served for two years at Andrews when I went to my two-star boss and told him that I needed to get back to the cockpit and asked to be relieved of this assignment to go to Armed Forces Staff College. He agreed, and I had an assignment to that school starting in January 1973.

Son Number Two Was Born (August 17, 1972)

We wanted to add another baby to our family. Unfortunately, every month was met with disappointment. Interestingly, we were back home again in Indiana for visit when B.J. began having the feeling that she might be pregnant. At that time, there was no drug store pregnancy test. We decided to check with Dad's high school classmate who was a doctor in local town. We had to wait to see if the rabbit died; and it did. We were elated that B.J. was pregnant and we were looking forward to this baby's arrival. Doug is named after his mother's and his paternal grandmother's maiden names. Douglas Taylor Watson joined our family on August 17, 1972. It seems that having three last names haven't slowed him down at all. This pregnancy was more difficult for B.J. She was anemic and had to have six massive shots of iron. We were blessed that both she and Doug were healthy and continue to be. Doug was a great baby, seldom cried and created few problems.

Even with the early promotion, our AF pay in the Washington, D.C. area was a little short. B.J. was offered a job in a downtown D.C. office of a travel agency where she could have used her Braniff and travel agency experience. When we analyzed the cost of her driving or commuting, clothes, lunches, taxes, and day care, her income would be less than the cost. She was much more valuable as a "Stay-At-Home-Mom" with two boys than with a professional career. To make up some of the shortfall, I taught flying at the Aero Club. We also rented the Aero Club airplanes to travel around the East Coast. The civilian flying time was a good start to my post-retirement flying.

One of the blessings of living in the D.C. area was the opportunity to visit the museums, monuments and halls of government. When Mom and Dad visited us, our Indiana Congressman invited us to lunch in the

House of Representatives Cafeteria and gave us a tour of the Capitol Building.

Another blessing was that our dear friends from Ramstein, Andrea and Lino DeMichelli, had preceded us to the D.C. area. He was assigned to the Pentagon and they lived about twenty miles away in a high-rise apartment in Arlington, Virginia. Once when B.J. and Derek were visiting them, B.J. and Andrea were chatting when the elevator door opened, Derek walked into the elevator and the women saw him just as the door closed. Panic ensued. They each took separate elevators checking each floor. When B.J. got to the first floor and the elevator opened, a man was standing there holding Derek's hand. He asked, "Are you looking for someone?" Yes, indeed she was.

Lino and Andrea preceded us on another assignment. This time to Armed Forces Staff College. They gave us a good briefing as to what to expect and they placed a flyer on the bulletin board advertising our house. A Navy officer and family bought our house saving us significant realtor fees.

Armed Forces Staff College in Norfolk, VA (1973)

AFSC, as it is known, was a six-month school for middle ranking officers of all services and international officers. I was a new Major when we arrived. After the long hours at Andrews AFB, I was happy to have a less strenuous schedule with time to be home with B.J., Derek and our new son, Doug.

The school was a great history lesson with the opportunity to study international affairs with international and inter-service officers. Their perspectives were fostered from a much different background than mine. Some of them had been involved in the situations we studied. The education received was a fantastic melding of theoretical and practical. In addition, we learned about each other's respective services giving us a good foundation for integrating the various military services as our careers progressed.

A friend from our church in Oxen Hill, Maryland had become commander of the large naval base in Norfolk. His wife and B.J. had been together in the church choir. He called inviting us and a few of our friends for a fishing trip on the "Captain's Gig", the boat assigned to the commander. We took two couples and kids for an afternoon of fishing on the Chesapeake Bay. With help from the crew, we caught about 60 flounder. Returning home, we cleaned them and gave most of them to friends and enjoyed a large community fish fry.

Since the school was only six months long, we began wondering about our follow-on assignments. Normally, graduates would go to a staff job to take advantage of the lessons of the staff school. However, I had just left a staff and was itching to get back into the cockpit. I knew the head of USAF assignments and gave him a call and explained my concern to get back to flying. He understood but made no commitment. Soon I received orders to the F-111A at Nellis AFB, Las Vegas, NV. Nellis is the home of the USAF Fighter Pilot just as Top Gun is the home of the Navy Fighter Pilot. I was excited to get there and start flying.

As we were packing for Nellis, we received new orders diverting us to Mountain Home AFB, ID, in the newest model of the F-111, the "F" model. Fortunately, our household goods had not been shipped and we made a smooth transition. One of my AFSC classmates had a pop-up tent trailer that he needed transported to Colorado. Since we were going through Colorado to visit B.J.'s parents and had a new Suburban, we volunteered to tow it for him if we could sleep in it. He agreed, and we enjoyed it on the way across the country. In Indiana, our boys talked Grandma and Grandpa Watson into spending the night camping in their backyard. I think the grandparents were quite happy to be back in their beds after one night in the camper discussing the stars with their grandsons.

After delivering the camper, we spent a few days with B.J.'s parents and other relatives. It was the first time they could see Doug, now almost a year old. Soon we were back on the road to Idaho.

Chapter 10: Back to the Cockpit

Mountain Home AFB, Idaho and the F-111F (1973-1976)

It was a two-day drive from Colorado Springs, and we arrived in the town of Mountain Home, Idaho in the afternoon. We were immediately unimpressed. The town was small and located a few miles off the interstate, not in the mountains. We were later to learn that many years before, the town had been in the mountains until the railroad came to the Snake River Valley. Consequently, they moved the town to the railroad, but didn't change the town's name.

Mountain Home AFB is the base where I picked up our RF-4Cs on the way to Vietnam about seven years earlier. It is located about 10 miles west of the town on a small road through the plains surrounded by sage brush. After driving a few minutes with nothing in sight, B.J. asked with concern in her voice, "Where are you taking me?" As we came over a little hill, she could see the base water tower on the horizon and began to cry. She had enjoyed living in Germany, Washington, and Norfolk and didn't see any of those features here. However, we were both to learn that God brought us to the desert just as He had brought many others for millennia to get their (and now our) attention.

We moved into a duplex on base. Our next-door neighbors were Lt. Colonel Bob and Kitty Osbourne. They were wonderful Christian people with two lovely daughters. When we pulled into the drive, we saw that they had a travel trailer like the RVs we had considered. After some discussion with them, Bob introduced us to his dealer, and we bought one like his. But before it and our Suburban were wired and ready for delivery, we had to go Fairchild AFB near Spokane, Washington to the altitude chamber. There aircrews learn the physiology of high-altitude flight including "explosive decompression" and hypoxia. Since we were in Idaho, we decided to borrow some camping equipment and camp in a tent on our way there and back. It was a lovely trip. However, as I drove the tent pegs into the hard, rocky, mountainous terrain, I decided the price was worth the ease and comfort of camping in the trailer.

Upon our return to Mountain Home, we received our household goods and began settling into our new house and the base. Finally, the Suburban was modified to pull the camping trailer and the trailer was delivered. We loaded it up with clothes and non-perishable food to enable us to quickly load fresh water and perishables to get on the road to the mountains when the schedule permitted. We took a one-night shake-down trip to a local campground to confirm that we were ready, and we were.

Since the F-111F was new, initial training had not been set up at Mountain Home. We had to go to Nellis AFB in Las Vegas for three weeks to get the necessary training. We decided to take the whole family in our new camping trailer, live in it in a Las Vegas campground while I went to school, and enjoy our time together. Our first night on the road, we stopped in a small town in Nevada. At the restaurant we remembered that it was Doug's first birthday. The waitress was very kind and insisted that he have a celebration. She came back with a stale cupcake and one candle. We sang *"Happy Birthday"* and split the cupcake four ways.

Arriving in Las Vegas, we found a campground with a swimming pool near Nellis. Since it was summer in Vegas, it was very dry and hot. The swimming pool became the respite for all of us. Even though Doug had just celebrated his first birthday, he was ready for the pool and would jump off the side into my arms. As he progressed and began to paddle, I would let him fall under water. Soon he was swimming. Several ladies around the pool thought I was an abusive dad by letting him go under water. However, his swimming ability quickly improved, and he is still a great swimmer. Many years later his swimming ability became a critical asset to both he and me receiving our deep-sea SCUBA certifications.

Signing into the class, I learned that we would only receive academic training for the F-111A. While it was the same airframe as the F-111F, the similarity soon ended. The F-111F that I would fly had the newest computers and much bigger engines than the F-111A. We learned the basic elements of the airframe, and the avionics were left to be taught at Mountain Home. After three weeks, we were headed back to Idaho.

The classes in Idaho concentrated on learning the computers, avionics, and differences between what the F-111A in Nellis and what we would actually fly in the F-111F at Mountain Home. The computers were the biggest change. The F-111A had older analog computers. Our computers were a combination of analog and digital with a conversion set that allowed the different computers to work together. Essentially, we had two of the same computers as the three that took men to the moon.

Our navigational system was about 10 times more accurate than the best in the RF-4C that I had flown before. The terrain following system of the RF-4C only gave us flight director guidance which the pilot had to manually follow. The system in the F-111 flew the airplane as if it was on autopilot. This huge improvement dramatically increased both the performance and safety of flying at 400 feet above the ground in mountainous terrain at night. Our attack radar was similarly more effective than previous models. There was a simulator at Mountain Home, but it was an A-Model and lacked the sophistication of the F-Model. Nonetheless, we soon were flying the airplane. When compared to the RF-4C that I had flown for about five years, moving to the F-111F was like moving from a Beetle to a Cadillac with a hemi-engine.

The F-111 series was characterized by its ability to sweep its wings. It was the fastest fighter in the Air Force and could exceed the speed of sound at sea level. We swept the wings forward for takeoff and landing and back to go supersonic. Sweeping the wings also gave us the opportunity to configure the airplane for the most efficient flying regardless of speed or altitude. We also carried more fuel than other fighters. In simulated combat with F-4s, we escaped by accelerating and running them low on fuel.

The F111F with Mountain Home AFB markings

Because of my extensive experience flying the RF-4C at low level, much of it at night, the transition to the F-111F was easy. Initially, I flew with an instructor pilot then with instructor navigators. A new subject came with the F-111: Nuclear weapon operations. Having the capacity to load nuclear bombs carries with it a high responsibility and the necessity for additional checks and balances. A special academic class and flight line indoctrination was required. We would only fly with nukes when directed by National Command Authority. However, we had to be trained and qualified for that contingency.

I was blessed to fly with many absolutely superior navigators and officers. Some had come from the Strategic Air Command flying B-52s and a few from the supersonic B-58. They brought extensive experience in navigation and bomb delivery. I quickly learned to rely on their expertise in all flight conditions, including night, weather, in the mountains.

The F-111F had a very long range and could drop a variety of bombs. A normal mission would be two to three hours in length to a bombing range where we would drop six or more small bombs with the same aerodynamic properties of the real, larger ones. The smaller practice bombs had a small explosive charge in the front of the bomb. When it hit the ground, a large puff of smoke was created. Towers on the bombing range could triangulate the location of the smoke to score the distance the bomb hit or missed the intended target. Periodically, we would simulate dropping nuclear weapons from higher altitudes. The high-altitude simulation used a radio tone from our airplane that drove a ground-based computer and plotter that scored our hits and misses.

After about a year, my navigator and I were selected to be one of two crews assigned to a Strategic Air Command (SAC) Bomb Competition. We were proud to be in the Tactical Air Command (TAC) flying fighters and looked down our noses at SAC and the bombers. Unfortunately, our arrogance would turn to bite us during the real competition. We would use our F-111s against the SAC B-52s and the British RAF Vulcan bombers. We flew a two and half hour high and low altitude route with a target in each of those legs. We didn't drop bombs, only the tone that we had used before to electronically score the bombs impact.

As we had in Royal Flush, we practiced almost every night. My job was to do the flight planning and keep a steady platform. Ray had to find the target using our inertial navigator and the attack radar. He often used radar returns that were easily identifiable and offset from the target. He could lock on that offset, update the inertial navigation system and the attack radar on those known coordinates, then the computers would slew the crosshairs to the target which was often unobservable on radar. In that case, we had to drop on the offset direction and distance from an observable radar return. We were supported by the crews and staff at Mountain Home.

The four-star commander of the Tactical Air Command was known to be gruff. He came to our base for a briefing about how we would win this competition. We briefed him on our attack plan, and he approved. Much like a football team going away to training camp, we deployed to Whiteman AFB near Kansas City, Missouri to finalize our practice and our game plan.

On the first night of the competition we took off confident that we would win the competition. A timing error caused us to be a little behind schedule. No problem, I lit the afterburners and accelerated to catch up. As we flew the route, Ray seemed relaxed that he had everything under control. However, on the low-level target, he was less confident. The target was not observable, and he had to use an offset that we had seen on previous practice missions, but it didn't seem quite right. We had to drop the tone regardless of confidence. Completing the mission, we landed at Barksdale AFB, Louisiana where all competitors would assemble to debrief the first mission and launch the second the following night. Upon arriving, we were met by the team captain with bad news. We had missed the second target. The second night went better, but not good enough to win the competition. We were embarrassed and disappointed. When we landed back home, only one person was there to meet us. B.J. welcomed us home whether we were a winner or not. She has always been my best fan, cheerleader and supporter.

We spent many hours going over the radar tapes to determine where we went wrong. We finally decided that the Inertial Navigation System (INS) had drifted about a mile even though Ray had updated it. Additionally, the radar offset that we had practiced must have been a portable metal building or large tractor that had moved. The combination of the INS drift and Ray being unable to find the primary offset resulted in the missed target. Several lessons were learned.

The following year our wing was invited to again participate in the bombing combination. Ray and I were one crew and we had two other crews. We worked closely with the other crews to pick radar observable offsets and INS updates to avoid the mistakes of the previous year. The competition crew was to be randomly selected and the mission flown from home base. All three of us practiced very diligently and were ready. Ray and I weren't selected, but the crew that was selected did great and our team won the competition. I was bummed that we didn't get a second chance but was happy the other crew won for our team.

Earlier I mentioned a Brigadier General at Andrews AFB that had been a mentor. I continued to stay in touch with him in the intervening two years. He called me saying he would like to come to Mountain Home to fly the F-111F with me so that he could better understand its capabilities. He was now a Major General assigned to the Organization of the Joint Chiefs of Staff (OJCS) in the Pentagon.

The flight was arranged, and I would be his instructor pilot for the flight. On the day of the arrival, I met with him and began to give him ground instruction and a short flight in the simulator. That evening he came to the house for dinner and was wonderful playing with the boys. Again, he suggested that Derek should hit us up for a Big Mac.

We flew on the second day of his visit. The mission was the same mission the other crews would be flying that day. We took off from Mountain Home flying a preplanned hour-long low-level flight around Idaho. We flew at 500 feet above the terrain at 480 knots ground speed (about 550mph). As we were finishing the low-level portion, I saw a snow shower on our attack radar a few miles in front of us. I asked him to engage the automatic terrain following radar system and descend to 400 feet. As we entered the snow shower no longer in visual contact ahead or even the ground, the airplane automatically turned onto the bombing range. We broke out of the snow a few miles before the target. I made a small correction on the radar and released the bomb. The crew in the range tower scored it as a direct hit. He was very impressed with the all-weather accuracy of the airplane.

After de-briefing our flight he said that it was time for me to move on and that the Chairman of the Joint Chiefs was interested in getting more operationally oriented officers on his staff. He made no other commitment to me as he left to go back to Washington. Interestingly, the Chairman had been the commander of the Air Force System Command at Andrews AFB when I was there. I often represented my boss at sat at the table during the command morning meetings. At one point I was interviewed to be his aide. Perhaps he remembered me from that time.

Life in Idaho

Despite the initial disappointment while driving into the base, we enjoyed living in Idaho and the varied outdoor activities there. We skied, fished, hunted, and camped in our travel trailer in the mountains near Boise, McCall, and Sun Valley.

We took a wonderful trip in our camping trailer with our duplex-mate family in their trailer. We went through Jackson Hole to Glacier National Park and to Banff and Lake Louise, Canada. We stayed a few days in Banff then pressed westward across the Canadian Rockies to Seattle. Along the way we say lots of Canadian wildlife and Derek fell in love with the big horn sheet. We stopped at one glacier and had a summer-time snow ball fight. Arriving in Seattle, we left the two trailers at a gas station and loaded all eight of us into our Suburban for a ferry trip to Victoria, Canada. We toured the local area and were enthralled with the Butchart Gardens. We then loaded back in our car, took the ferry and returned to the trailers in Seattle. The final leg of our trip was along the Colombia River, then the Snake River back to Mountain Home. It is unfortunate that the boys were very young and don't remember much of the trip. But we did have a valuable family time. Derek does remember having the snow ball fight on a glacier and the Big Horn Sheep that we saw along the road.

We took a hike through the mountains above Banff
Doug had the best seat

We loved camping in Idaho and wanted to do more. We sold our travel trailer and bought a small motor home. The motor home was especially easy to use. B.J. took the boys and a couple of their friends to a movie in Boise, about an hour from the base, to celebrate Derek's birthday. It was a wonderful time for all. We also enjoyed taking it to the mountains, fly fishing and just enjoying the outdoors as a family.

Winters in Idaho were spent either skiing or wishing we were. B.J. and I signed up with the Youth Center to chaperon a school bus that would take kids from the base to Bogus Basin, just north of Boise, Idaho. Derek could ride for free if he sat with us on the bus. Doug was relegated to a baby sitter at home. Because we were often at Bogus Basin, we became well known with the child care center and ski patrol, the later due to minor injuries of the kids on our bus. We could hire a teenage girl to get Derek from child care and give him ski lessons on the Bunny Slope. When the lesson was over, she would take him back to child care. Toward the end of the season we were seeing him ski down the slopes, usually well ahead of his teacher. The following year, Derek learned to check himself out of Child Care and ski and we would see him on the slopes. When he got cold, he would check himself back into Child Care. The last year we were in Idaho, we chaperoned for 8 weeks. But in the Spring, Derek (age 8) could ride the bus alone, ski and come home on the bus. Of course, we knew the chaperons and they watched him as had we. However, I cannot now imagine allowing a child of that age doing the things he not only did but excelled in doing.

In the Spring of 1976, we decided we should take a road trip with the boys. We set out in the motor home by going north along the Snake River until we got to the Columbia River, then followed it West to the Pacific Ocean. It was the reverse trip that we had previously taken in our travel trailer following our journey through Canada. We loved stopping to see the beautiful scenery and animals along the way. We stopped in Eugene, OR to visit friends who had been stationed with us at Mountain Home. From there we headed straight to the Pacific and turned South following the Pacific Coast all the way to San Francisco. Enroute we camped in the Redwood Forest with a huge herd of elk. Moving on we stopped in the Napa Valley wine country for a day or so.

Our next stop at the Presidio in San Francisco was eventful. As we were resupplying the camper and enjoying an evening in a real bed, I called back to Mountain Home to be told we had received an assignment to the Organization of the Joint Chiefs of Staff in the Pentagon, and we were to report as soon as possible.

We decided to continue the trip to Los Angeles and Disneyland for the boys. Again, we made stops along the way to buy fresh vegetables, take in the scenery, and just enjoy being together as a family. At one stop, I forgot to pull in the step. As we were winding our way along the Big Sur Highway, the step side-swiped the guard rail and immediately got our attention as to the impressive drop off just beyond the guard rail. B.J. quickly left her seat and retracted the step.

After a momentous stop at Disney Land and a visit with B.J.'s cousin, we turned east to the Grand Canyon. B.J. wanted to fix dinner as we were coming out of the Grand Canyon Park and started a meat loaf in the camper oven. However, given all the twists and turns of the canyon road, it spilled over and began to smoke. Smoke was pouring outside the motor home, but we couldn't see it in the camper. Passing motorists could see it and began honking at us. We stopped, found the source, and ate the meat loaf before we attracted more attention. While the oven was crusted with the spill, the meat loaf was delicious.

Our next stop was at the junction of the four states of Colorado, Utah, Arizona and New Mexico. We took the classic picture of all of us standing on the plaque with each of us in a different state. From there we went to Colorado Springs to visit B.J.'s family for a couple of days. Her mom and dad joined us and continued our odyssey through Colorado and Utah to Idaho. B.J.'s parents stayed a few days before returning home to Colorado and we started making arrangements to move to the Washington area.

Our time at Mountain Home started with tears as we drove into the base. However, our three years there were filled with professional growth, family activities and significant commitment to following Jesus Christ. A major turning point was B.J. accepting Jesus as her Savior and Lord. She had been attending church but had never turned her life over to Jesus. At Mountain Home she joined a Bible study with our chaplain's wife. After one study, Nancy asked her if she would like to accept Jesus and commit her life to Him. She said yes; they prayed together; B.J. was Born Again.

That evening B.J. recommended that we start a Bible Study with a few couples whose wives had attended the Ladies Bible Study with her. I explained that I had accepted Jesus as Savior and Lord as a young teenager and had been in Sunday School and Church all the years since. But, being a fine husband, if she wanted a Bible study, I would attend with her (note the sarcasm). We started the study with about five couples rotating the studies and meetings between homes. Our walk with the Lord and our knowledge of the Bible began to grow by leaps and bounds and was the basis for our continued Christian walk and growth. Thankfully, B.J. listened to the Holy Spirit and recognized what I needed more than I. Of the original five couples, three went to seminary and became pastors, one was a representative with The Navigators, and we have continued to lead Bible Studies and become leaders in our churches. We had studied the Holy Spirit and His gifts. In one study, we each prayed to be filled with the Holy Spirit. This was a major turning point in our Christian walk. The manifestation of the Gifts of The Spirit became more obvious as we continued to study and pray for His direction in our lives.

Our time at Mountain Home was fulfilling in my professional career, our family time and in our Christian walk. We were sad to leave our friends at Mountain Home, but excited to get on with the new assignment. As a going away party, the on-base Chapel staff asked B.J. to sing a solo and honored us with a short reception following the service. Everyone was very kind in expressing their sadness of our departure and we would certainly miss them as well.

We left the reception, rushed to the parking lot, hooked up our VW Bug, named Beep-Beep, by the boys. The motorcycle was loaded on the motor home and we headed down the road.

Chapter 11: The Pentagon: The Joys and the Challenges

Destination: The Pentagon (1976-1980)

Due to the extended goodbyes at Mountain Home, we were a couple of hours behind schedule. As night approached, we stopped for fuel in Jackson Hole, Wyoming and B.J. arranged the beds for the night. The boys slept in the king-sized overhead bed that was above the driver's seat. Our bed was in the back. Consequently, I could continue to drive while they slept. The gas attendant told us to continue toward Yellowstone Park and we would find a scenic pullout where we could get some sleep.

B.J. and the boys went to sleep, and I drove another hour or so and found the scenic overlook, pulled over and climbed into bed. We had been told that it was illegal to park overnight in the pullout and that the Highway Patrol would probably wake us up. Sure enough, just before dawn we were awakened with a loud banging noise on the door. I opened it and said, "Good Morning" to the officer. She said, "You have got to move on." I replied, "Yes ma'am." B.J. and the boys began getting dressed and I took our dog for a short run. Returning to the camper, I assembled everyone on our big bed in the back, then opened the curtains for them to get the full effect of the rising sun shining brightly on the beautiful Teton Mountains. We had parked in the same scenic overlook that is the location used to take the tourist pictures.

We headed down the road to Yellowstone arriving at the main gate just as it was opening. The ranger suggested we go to any of the campgrounds and find a spot since they were first come, first served. Just as we arrived at the first campground, a truck with a large trailer RV pulled out leaving perfect room for our MH and VW. We disconnected the VW and spent the day driving it through the park. Thanks to the unceremonious awakening, we were early to everything Yellowstone had to offer. We arrived at Old Faithful before the crowds arrived and toured the park with little traffic. We would have loved to stay longer, but we were on a mission.

The next day we continued to Mount Rushmore and a stop to see the four former presidents dramatically sculpted into the mountain. We continued our odyssey across the Badlands to St. Louis to visit one of my aunts and uncles. B.J. was born in St. Louis and she had the opportunity to tell the boys about her early childhood there. We loaded back in the MH and on to Graysville, IN where Grandparents Watson and brother Bill and family were waiting. It had been a wonderful, but somewhat tiring trip. We were glad to be back to my childhood home and the hospitality of Mom and Dad.

After a few days with them, we left the boys with grandparents and B.J. and I continued to Northern Virginia in the MH, motorcycle and VW. Earlier I mentioned that Charlotte Phillips had been a couple of years ahead of me at Graysville High School. After she graduated, she became an Air Force Nurse and married another Air Force officer, Dennis Politano. After retirement they settled down in Oxon Hill, MD. We had connected with them when we were at our previous assignment at Andrews AFB. They were very kind to offer us a place to stay until we found a home. B.J. and I quickly accepted. We put the motor home and motorcycle up for sale and they quickly sold giving us cash for the down payment on our home.

House hunting was hectic. Since we had lived in the DC area only four years before, we were familiar with the metropolitan area. We knew we didn't want to live in Maryland and concentrated our search in Northern Virginia. After several days, we found a nice home in Kings Park West, Fairfax, VA. It was close to the Beltway which improved my commute to the Pentagon, was affordable (almost), and had bus transportation to the Pentagon and downtown. With the home contracted, B.J. flew back to Indiana and I stayed to begin work and campout with the Politanos.

I was pressed to sign in with the Organization of the Joint Chiefs of Staff (OJCS) at the Pentagon. The OJCS works directly for the Chairman of the Joint Chiefs to integrate the various inputs from the Army, Navy, Marines and Air Force as well as the different intelligence agencies. As mentioned earlier, the then JCS Chairman, USAF General Brown, wanted more operational experience on the staff. Consequently, I was assigned to the Operations Directorate, Office of Current Operations. In short, we worked on what was happening at any given moment, anywhere in the world. I was quickly introduced to the National Military Command Center, National Military Intelligence Center, and the National Reconnaissance Center. Briefings to gain access to those centers took two or three days and special identification badges were introduced in addition to the badge to enter the Pentagon.

With in-processing briefings completed and security clearances in place, I could go back to Indiana and pick up the family. Since the motor home and motorcycle were sold, I asked B.J. to look for a car large enough for us to finish the move to Virginia and adequate for carpooling. She and Dad found us a gently used Ford Station Wagon that met our needs and was affordable (almost). We loaded it up with kids and suitcases and hit the road again.

The family's arrival in Virginia meant closing on the house, enrolling in school, and learning the challenges of living in the nation's capital. We were blessed that the Politanos hosted us until we could receive our household goods that were shipped from Idaho. Things happened quickly. We closed on the house and the movers arrived the next day. Derek, our older son, enrolled in the King's Park Elementary School and could walk to school. Doug was still a year too young for kindergarten. I found a car pool from our neighborhood to the Pentagon that served well for the next four years.

Life in the Nation's Capital:

Our highest priority when we arrived in a new place was to find a church. My upbringing had been as a Methodist. While we were living on base, we attended the chapel. Now back in a civilian environment, we began looking for a Methodist Church. There was a nice looking one only a couple of miles from our house, so we decided to try it out. However, in the first Sunday School Class, the teacher asked how we would modify our Christian walk when we went back to work on Monday. Our commitment to Jesus Christ did not permit a Sunday religion that would be modified to fit the work culture on Monday. That church failed its first test and it didn't get a second chance.

As we met people in our daily activities, we asked them for church suggestions. Finally, someone recommended the Metropolitan Christian Center. They explained that it was charismatic, believed in the entire Bible, and the pastor was excellent. We tried it the next Sunday and stayed there for the next four years. We also found that they had a Christian School associated with the church. We transferred Derek and Doug to the school with B.J. becoming the quintessential chauffeur.

We did find that the teaching from the pulpit was excellent and Derek did well in school. However, Doug had challenges with the kindergarten teacher. She just couldn't handle what we now call hyperactivity and she clearly demonstrated that she did not like him. Fortunately, we found that the pre-kindergarten teacher was extremely well qualified, and Doug and she took a mutual liking to each other. Moving Doug to her class was the answer. The next year the problem teacher left the school. We were very active in the church with B.J. singing, including solos, with the choir. While we didn't have Elders, I could have been considered one because of my varying roles there.

We had always liked sports cars and having been promoted to Lt. Colonel gave us some disposable income. The VW Bug brought from Idaho was sold and I surprised B.J. with a new Datsun 280Z. However, there was a problem. When the Ford wasn't available, she had been carpooling several kids to the Christian Center School and the 280Z was smaller than the VW. The Z-Car was a 2+2 with a small back seat, she could put Derek in the front seat and cram several smaller kids into the back seat with one or two overflowing into the hatchback. In retrospect, it wasn't the safest approach. However, there was never an accident and the infamous Beltway presented no problems to B.J. or the kids. The rules today would have found us criminally negligent. Fortunately, all is well that ends well.

Sometimes we miss the trees for the forest. That was the case at the Christian Center. We were involved in the school, choir and other activities and thought that the full picture of the operations of the church and school were going well. However, the singular events weren't. Doug wasn't progressing at his full potential and there were leadership issues just below the senior pastor. There were subtle indications that have become more obvious as time progressed. I should have taken a more critical look at some of the seemingly minor individual issues that were the result of deeper, more critical, spiritual problems.

Fortunately, we had selected a nice neighborhood. We had good neighbors and the carpool to the Pentagon stopped in front of the house. Soon the boys were on swim and soccer teams. The Braddock Road Sports Club had over a thousand members involved in dozens of sports throughout the entire year. Our boys concentrated on soccer and were on teams named after the characters in the "Peanuts" comic strip. Both became very proficient with Derek a Striker and Doug a goalie. Soccer gave them a good foundation in sports and teamwork that would benefit them throughout their future.

The biggest advantage to living in the DC Metropolitan Area is the proximity to history, politics and "what's happening now." One of best excursions was a July 5th Celebration. Yes, I know it is a July 4th Celebration. However, on this particular year, there was a huge rainstorm on the 4th and the fireworks were rescheduled to the 5th. B.J. loaded a backpack with snacks and water and she and the boys met me at the Pentagon. We took the subway to the Capitol. We found a seat on the west stairs leading down from the Capitol. The boys ran around before we had the snacks. The National Symphony began playing just below us. As Arthur Fiedler raised his hands directing the "Stars and Stripes Forever," the sky erupted between his arms with the fireworks lighting up the entire Mall. Fantastic, and we were up close and personal for the entire presentation of music and explosives. As the end approached, people started moving down the Mall to subway stations. I grabbed the family and we ran in the opposite direction, up Capitol Hill to get to the station. We were among the first on board and had seats. The train quickly filled. As we progressed toward the Pentagon, all the stations were full of people. They didn't even open the doors at the other stations since there was no room on the train. We got to the Pentagon in minimum time, walked to the car, and were home in less than an hour after the final boom.

As could be imagined, we had many family members visit during our four years in DC. Most of the time we gave them directions to the tourist site they wanted to see and headed them out the door. We had other priorities that prevented us from accompanying them. However, if they wanted to go to the Air and Space Museum, I usually could get the time off to be their personal escort.

Another benefit was being able to attend some of the big celebrations. Our Indiana Congressman Myers got us four tickets to Jimmy Carter's inauguration. It was very cold and a zoo of people all trampling each other to get to the viewing area. Even though we had special tickets, the police couldn't control the pressing crowd to allow us to enter. Eventually, they quit trying to restrict entrance to ticket holders and it was chaotic. The crush of people was scary, and we were careful to not fall and get trampled. We had invited another couple and we were able to stick together to get a view of the podium as the newly inaugurated President Carter began to speak. We decided to bail out before the speeches were complete and the crowd surged from the Capitol Grounds. We found a warm restaurant. Good Decision.

We loved the four seasons of living in Northern Virginia. In the fall we would go to the mountains and enjoy the changing colors of the leaves. Another advantage is that many of our Air Force friends were stationed in the DC area at one time or another. One year, we loaded our family and our friends from Germany, Charlie and Sindy Schwab and their two girls, in our station wagon and drove to the orchards west of DC. We had a wonderful time picking apples, picnicking and just visiting as the kids expended energy running the hills. Arriving home B.J. and Sindy baked apple pies and canned apples that lasted several months.

On a vacation trip to the Shenandoah Mountains, we purchased a time share cabin at Bryce Mountain. It had a golf course, lake, and ski area, and it had a runway; all our fun things in one resort. One year we took the Schwab family to our little cabin for a ski trip. Coincidently, the Winter Olympics were being held in Lake Placid. After a day of skiing, we opened the hide-a-bed in the living room and all eight of us flopped on the bed to watch the US beat the Russians in Hockey. "Do you believe in miracles?"

Another memorable trip was with good friends John and Gwyn Underwood. We had known them in a previous assignment at Andrews AFB in Maryland. They owned a large yacht that was berthed on the Potomac River near the DC Airport. John wanted to move it from there to Annapolis and asked us to go along. We were happy to be invited and we joined them and another family for the trip that would go down the Potomac from Washington then up the Chesapeake Bay to Annapolis. It was Memorial Day and we were expecting clear, warm weather. We packed shorts and swim suits in anticipation of getting an early tan. But the opposite occurred. It was cold, misty, and windy. The cruise down the Potomac was relatively calm in the protected areas of the river. We spent the night in a harbor at the confluence of the Potomac and Chesapeake. As we were tying the boat to the pier a gentleman asked John the length of his yacht. I have always remembered John's answer: "If you are washing it, it is too long. If you are in the ocean during a storm, not nearly long enough." In many ways, that sums up life. Much of our life circumstances depend upon our perspective and on our situation at that time.

The next day we continued into more open waters of the Chesapeake Bay and the North Winds kicked up. We were heading into rough water with the larger waves going over the top of the yacht's flying bridge. Soon several people, including John, were feeling ill. John asked me to take the helm and navigate us toward Annapolis. I had never piloted a large boat, let alone his yacht. However, looking at his instruments and the map, I could see the channel was laid out with the buoys being distinctively colored and/or numbered well and depicted on the map. In my aviation mind, navigation along the marked channel was much like an airway marked with VORs guiding aircraft along the airway. I used my wrist stop watch to determine the time between two buoys. Measuring the distance between the buoys on the map, I calculated our speed through the water. I could then apply our speed to the distance to the next buoy that was beyond sight due to fog and rain. It worked well. The waves remained rough. Smaller boats were being tossed up, down, and around. At one point, B.J. grabbed my arm and started pointing at the galley. The bouncing and lurching of the boat had dislodged the microwave and it was about to fall out of the cabinet. I called John and he jumped down into the galley and secured the microwave before it fell to the floor. Doug and I were the only ones not to get sick. He slept on the co-pilot's seat with his head on my lap. The wind through the cockpit was cool and he enjoyed the snooze, only waking as we entered calmer water approaching the dock. Everyone was happy to be out of the rough Chesapeake.

We loved living in Northern Virginia even though it was expensive, and the Pentagon job was very demanding. Thirteen years later we would return to the area; this time I was a civilian working for an aviation services company.

Working at the Organization of the Joint Chiefs of Staff (OJCS), The Pentagon (1976-1980)

As mentioned earlier, I was assigned to the Current Operations Division of the Operations Directorate, OJCS. Just as the name implies, we were responsible for military operations anywhere in the world.

The individual Services of Air Force, Army, Navy, Marine Corps and Coast Guard execute the orders of the President and Secretary of Defense as passed down by the Joint Chiefs of Staff. Our division developed contingency plans and options, then wrote the orders that were carried out by the Services. In general, if it was on the front page of the paper or TV Nightly News, we were involved.

Upon my arrival at the Pentagon in 1976 during the Ford Administration, there was high strain along the Korean Demilitarized Zone (DMZ). That crisis became critical when the U.S. Army attempted to cut down a tree that obstructed its view of the northern portion of the DMZ. The North Korean Army (NKA) didn't want that to happen and two American officers were beaten to death with the blunt end of axes after they ignored the North Koreans' order to stop. Clearly, that would not stand. A plan was developed and presented to the JCS and Secretary of Defense that the Army would use necessary force to cut the tree and confirm our rights within the DMZ. The plan was approved and would be executed the next day. I was summoned to the National Military Command Center where our team had live radio coming from the action. As we were listening to our troops cutting the tree, we heard them say a truck of NKA troops had arrived and were getting out of the truck. I said a prayer asking the Lord to tell the NKA troops to get back in the truck and leave. The next report was that the troops were getting back into the truck and leaving. Praise the Lord for answered prayer. The tension was removed, the tree was cut, and both sides went back to the normal state of readiness. In the intervening years, the tension and mutual distrust between the United States and Korea has continued. Hopefully, negotiations beginning in 2018 to reduce the animosity and for North Korea to give up its nuclear weapons and intercontinental ballistic missiles will be successful.

President Carter became president only six months into my four-year tour. Initially he was to be the "People's President" and began his administration by carrying his own suitcase, implementing social programs, and avoiding international issues. Many of his actions were for what we now call "optics." Insiders reported that the suitcase was empty, his social programs were not implemented and his attempt at foreign policy was a failure. He was often viewed by foreign friends and adversaries as being weak and ineffectual. This perceived weakness in the international arena became temptation for potential foes to test him, thus the United States. His entire time in office (and mine too since we overlapped) was fraught with trials and testing. Each time a foreign power jabbed at the U.S., our Current Operations Division became involved. Moreover, in his later years President Carter wrote extensively against Israel and even got the Biblical references wrong.

Clearly, the most notable international failure during the Carter Administration occurred when the ayatollahs of Iran captured our embassy and imprisoned our personnel. One of those captured was a friend who only a few months before also had been assigned to the OJCS in the Plans Directorate.

The Operations Directorate was the obvious choice to lead the efforts to get our people released. I became the OJCS representative and manager of the nighttime Crisis Action Team (CAT) working on the overt plans for the release. Working with the individual Services, we drafted plans to relocate military forces to the region, contribute to the Department of State's negotiations, and plan military operations should they become necessary. A separate team developed the covert plans for "Operation Eagle Claw" that would plan the longest, most complex rescue mission ever attempted. It was tragic that the attempt failed when a blinding sandstorm cut visibility to zero resulting in a collision between rescuing aircraft.

The East/West Conflict continued with the Soviet Union testing President Carter often and all over the globe. The USSR was exploiting our challenges in Iran by pushing into other areas of Southwest Asia. In Libya, Muhammar Gadhafi was challenging the U.S. Navy and international shipping as he tried to expand his influence further into the Mediterranean Sea. And China was expanding its influence in the Western Pacific.

China, USSR, and other maritime countries often try to extend their influence and control beyond the internationally recognized limits. International law permits peaceful transit of waters outside of the recognized territorial limits. To enforce the Rights of Passage, the U.S. Navy periodically moves ships into these disputed waters. Similar surveillance is also conducted by USAF and Navy reconnaissance aircraft. Normally these exercises are conducted with the territorial country intercepting and shadowing but taking no overt action.

However, at one point, Gadhafi attempted to attack our ships by sending fighter aircraft out toward them. His aircraft were met by F-14s from the Mediterranean Fleet. The Libyan aircraft were destroyed with no damage to the U.S. Navy aircraft.

Perhaps the most bizarre project happened in our own hemisphere. I was the on-call duty officer sitting at home when the National Military Command Center (NMCC) called to tell me that there were reports that U.S. Congressman Leo Ryan had been killed in Guyana. If true, it would be our division that would prepare the appropriate orders to send a military plane there to recover his body. I jumped in our car and headed to the Pentagon. By the time I arrived in the NMCC, the reports were arriving of the "revolutionary suicide" of the adherents of Jim Jones. Peoples Temple leader Jones had instructed all his members to commit suicide by drinking poisoned punch. I activated the Terrorist Action Team to bring together previously appointed members from each of the Services to plan the follow-on action to bring Congressman Ryan's body back to the U.S. and determine what had happened in Jonestown. As we were to learn, 912 people, including 276 children, died from drinking poison-laced punch which had been pre-positioned to enable the cult members to commit suicide. Jones died from a gunshot to the head. Another six people died at the airport with Congressman Ryan. A year later at Air War College, I met the Air Force officer who had commanded the recovery of the dead bodies in his unit's helicopters. He could not believe the impact of stifling heat and decaying bodies. It was a tragedy of greatest proportions.

Of course, President Carter was noted for negotiating the Panama Canal to be transferred to the Panamanians. The Current Operations Division developed the alternatives to various treaty scenarios. While I was not directly involved in those efforts, I often was in the meetings that discussed the various treaty provisions that addressed U.S. forces in Panama. Ironically, about six years later I would become the Commander of the United States Air Force Southern Air Division and the 24th Composite Air Wing, both located at Howard Air Force Base in the Panama Canal Zone. More about that assignment and associated ironies later.

It was also rewarding to work closely with the best and brightest of the various Services. Together, we pushed paper, planned operations, and worried about which country would be the next to strike at the U.S. I also had the pleasure and privilege of working closely with brilliant general officers. Jerry O'Malley was the two-star USAF general Deputy Director of Operations. He became a mentor that taught me not only military operations, but also people skills. Several times he called me directly asking me to do specific projects and studies. I always briefed my supervisors but delivered the study products directly to him.

He called asking if I had a resume and my military personnel records. I told him that they were in the administrative files. He directed me to get them and deliver them to another Air Force general officer in the Chairman's office. I did. That general took the folders and immediately ran up the stairs. Unknown to me at the time, the Below-the-Zone selection committee for promoting officers to the rank of Colonel (O-6) was meeting. Subsequently, I have assumed my records were hand-carried into that committee. I arrived at the Pentagon with the rank of Major and left four years later as a Colonel-selectee, one of the youngest in the Air Force at that time.

My four years at the OJCS were demanding on me and our family. I had many 18-hour days, and a couple that were 24 hours. I traveled to Europe and Australia for major military exercises and planned the trip and travelled with the Deputy Secretary of Defense to Europe. Professionally, it was very rewarding.

However, the demands at home were equally challenging. My absence placed greater burdens on B.J. She did a fantastic job maintaining the family, continuing in the church choir, and being both Mom and Dad when I was gone. But it took a physical and emotional toll on her. We worked hard to keep the family properly grounded and focused. We always tried to have dinner together. However, the Iranian Revolution and capture of embassy and personnel made it nearly impossible to have time together for the last year we were in Washington. In many ways, B.J. was a single mom during that last year. Often, I left for the Pentagon before the boys awoke and returned after they were in bed. I would go up to their rooms when they were asleep and pray over them, telling the Lord that these were my sons, of whom I am very proud. I also told them the same thing.

One Spring morning when the boys were off from school, B.J. called and said, "Meet us at the River Entrance to the Pentagon. We are taking you to lunch." I said I couldn't leave, but she wisely insisted. At the appointed time I left The Building to find her in the 280Z, boys and dog sticking out of the windows, and a picnic basket in the hatch back. She drove us over to an area near the Jefferson Monument. We walked under the budding Cherry Trees, spread a blanket and had lunch. The boys threw the frisbee and ran with the dog while she and I had a very nice visit. It was a wonderful family moment captured in our memories during a time when there weren't many opportunities to be together. Thanks to her for again being insistent.

Toward the end of our tour, we were slated to go to a senior officer school. I had asked to attend the National War College in Washington, D.C. so that we could continue to live in Northern Virginia another year. However, the explanation was that I had been on the Joint Staff and out of the Air Force for four years, I needed to go to the Air War College to be "Re-Blued" and get back with other USAF officers.

We were glad to receive orders to the Air War College at Maxwell AFB, Alabama. We were desperately looking forward to leaving the OJCS to a much less demanding schedule, the opportunity to enjoy more family time, and the academic challenge of becoming a student.

As earlier mentioned, we had purchased a lovely home in the Northern Virginia suburbs and financed it using my Veteran's Benefit at 7 1/2% interest. While that interest rate seems astronomical today, during the Carter Administration some loans had gone to nearly 18%. Consequently, we found that we could sell the house for a higher price if we allowed the buyer to assume our VA Loan, which we did. By assuming our VA Loan, they could afford our house which they could not have afforded at the going interest rate. Sometimes things work out for the best for both us and them.

Chapter 12: Another Professional School: The Air War College

Leaving Virginia for Alabama

We shipped our household goods and loaded our 280Z and Ford Station Wagon and headed down the road toward Maxwell AFB near Montgomery, Alabama. In the days before cellular phones but with CB radios, we communicated between Mom with one son and the other son and me in separate cars. In the process of turning off an interstate, she called on the CB that our right rear tire was wobbling. Fortunately, we were near a Sears store and pulled into the garage to find that two lug bolts were broken, and another was about to fail. God's provision for us and her attention to our car prevented an almost certain major accident. Again, thank you Lord for caring for us.

We had rented a home in Prattville, Alabama from a friend we had known in the F-111 days in Idaho. After we went there to drop off some of our load, we headed to Maxwell AFB to stay in the visiting officers' quarters until we were settled in the rental house. As we wandered the Alabama back roads in the now darkness, B.J. missed a turn that I had taken. She had no idea where we were or how to get to Maxwell. Fortunately, we were within CB radio range and were able to find a common spot to rejoin the formation. As we say in the flying business, we were never lost, but we were temporarily disoriented.

The house was very comfortable and in a wonderful neighborhood. However, the schools in Prattville were not very good. We enrolled the boys in a church school near the house. In 1980 segregation was very much a factor and was only slightly better than our experience in Selma 16 years earlier. I coached the school's junior high basketball team and our son, Derek. I had the opportunity to talk to the team about the evil and hateful manner of some of the students treating the other race. Of course, we will never know the impact on the other kids, but our boys learned valuable life lessons.

One weekend, we drove the boys to Selma, AL. We showed them our previous little apartment, the BBQ shack, and the base where I had learned to fly. We also drove them across the Edmund Pettis Bridge and talked about the Martin Luther King march to Montgomery. Here, as in other places where we lived, we tried to relate the geography with the history lessons they were learning in school. The opportunity to teach them "on-the-ground" history has been very important in their transition to moving from school to school, often in the middle of the year. Obviously, they paid a penalty for leaving friends, familiar schools and comfortable situations. However, the lessons they learned in each of the new environments paid great benefits as they have aged.

It is extremely unfortunate that what was being discussed in their school in Prattville was wrongly prejudiced and clearly violated the Watson Family Values. The trip to Selma and their experience during the year in Prattville opened their eyes to the evil of segregation and how they could make a difference in integrating other people into their lives.

The Air War College (AWC) (1980-1981)

AWC, as it is known, is the USAF senior officer military school. The curriculum includes extensive studies of battles, international affairs, political environments, and potential situations that graduates might experience in their future careers. But it is also in a rather relaxed, academic environment with classes typically over about noon with independent study in the afternoon. For some, independent study meant golf. However, for me, it meant hurrying home to re-establish family relationships, sports with the boys, and shopping with B.J. My extra hours of studying were done at night when the boys were doing their homework.

Another intended aspect of AWC was to meet and learn from officers from other Services and from the International Services. We built close friendships with many of them, including a Nigerian Prince and wife who would later become a leader in their country. As mentioned earlier, one AWC classmate had commanded the recovery of the bodies from Jonestown. He and I had long conversations about how it was executed from both Washington and the field. Another classmate became the Deputy Commander for Operations of the USAF Military Airlift Command. After I had retired, I called him. I was directing the resupply of the Free Kuwait Air Force during Desert Shield/Storm. He provided critical coordination to resupply the Free Kuwaiti Forces.

My experience with the OJCS at The Pentagon was extremely valuable at AWC. I had been involved with the major projects of the past four years. Consequently, I brought a "Washington Perspective" to the classroom and I learned the "Operational Perspective" from my classmates. I did well in the classroom, with writing exercises, and led a paper-exercise very similar to the actual deployment exercise that I had chaired in Washington and executed in Europe. All of that together contributed to my being selected a "Distinguished Graduate."

B.J. and I had been very involved in small group Bible Studies for the past 6 years in Mountain Home and Virginia, primarily through Officers' Christian Fellowship (OCF). While other professional military schools had well-coordinated OCF presence, there was none at Maxwell. I asked OCF if I could start Bible Studies and received approval. I met each incoming member of AWC and the intermediate school, Air Command and Staff College, to invite them to a meeting to establish a network of Bible Studies. Ultimately, we had about a dozen studies at Maxwell by the time we left. Later OCF selected a representative to continue the work that we had started. In addition to our Bible Studies, I worked with the Air Force Chief of Chaplains to come to AWC to hold a baccalaureate service. We had known him and his wife in Washington and he was happy to accept the invitation. However, we had to hold the service in a church downtown since the school would not sponsor a religious activity. Clearly, there is a terrible misunderstanding of what the Constitution permits with respect to Freedom of Religion.

Typically, graduates of AWC would be assigned to a high-level assignment at a major command or the Air Staff in the Pentagon. However, I had just completed that type of assignment and wanted to get back in the cockpit. Soon I had orders to the A-10 at Myrtle Beach AFB, South Carolina. We were all very excited. I would be flying, and we would be living across the road from a world-famous beach. Life was looking good.

Chapter 13: Refreshed and Back to the Cockpit

On the Road Again to Myrtle Beach AFB, SC (1981)

We were happy to pack the household goods and load the cars for our next assignment. We drove to Indiana for a short visit then to Colorado Springs visiting family along the way. B.J. and the boys stayed in Colorado enjoying the mountains and reuniting with our dear friends the DeMichielis. I headed to Davis Monthan AFB in Tucson, AZ for A-10 training.

B.J. packed our two boys, her sister's son and the two DeMichieli boys and went to the Officers Christian Fellowship Retreat at Spring Canyon, CO. This is a fabulous facility high in the mountains with trails, a lake and fun things to do. The boys enjoyed fishing for trout in the lake but were a little too exuberant and fell out of the boat. Apart from being dunked in cold water, they enjoyed the experience. I joined them when I finished the A-10 training. After a visit a few years later, Doug would remain on the staff at Spring Canyon for the summer.

A-10 "Warthog"

A-10 training was at Davis Monthan AFB, AZ

The A-10 is officially named the "Thunderbolt II" after the P-47 WWII fighter. However, it is better known by its popular name, the "Warthog" because it is unattractive as compared to other fighters such as the F-4, F-15, F-16 and F-35. Its design suffered major criticism, both from the Air Force fighter pilots who wanted sexy, sleek looking fighters and the Congress who didn't know what they wanted. During its development, a congressman referred to the A-10 as a "turkey." The USAF general explained that it was a pretty good moniker, but not for what the congressman meant. The general explained that the turkey was an American icon, was an excellent hunter and that it was hard to kill. For the troops on the ground, it was a life saver. The 30mm Gatling gun produced high rate, accurate firepower. It could also carry precision guided munitions.

I was proud to fly the airplane. After a week or so of ground school and simulator training, I was in the airplane. Since it is single-seat with no instructor on board, the first takeoff is solo. An instructor in another A-10 flies in formation, watching every move, and coaching as necessary using the inter-flight radio. After a half dozen or so flights, I graduated and was cleared to go to Myrtle Beach to become fully combat ready in the airplane.

My training complete and families visited, we were back on the road to Myrtle Beach. The Wing Commander was very welcoming. However, the house he wanted us to have in the same cul-de-sac as the other senior officers wasn't yet available when we arrived. Unfortunately, we had to move into two adjoining rooms in the Visiting Officers' Quarters. That was not a good arrangement for active boys and their dog. They couldn't understand why we were there and not in the house that had been promised to us. And they couldn't understand why they had to be quiet and not run down the halls while the night crews were trying to sleep. Finally, we were able to move into "permanent" quarters and the boys started school.

My title was "Assistant Deputy Commander for Operations," the number two guy responsible for the day-to-day flying activities. My boss was a highly experienced officer and pilot and was instrumental in getting me properly oriented to my new responsibilities. I had been out of the cockpit for five years and the A-10 was significantly different than other airplanes I had previously flown, but I was loving it.

Early one evening I received a call from the weather office explaining that the hurricane that was forecast to miss us was now heading directly toward us. My boss was on travel, so I called the Wing Commander and asked him to meet me at the Weather Shop. We decided that we should evacuate the airplanes to England AFB, LA. In the next 24 hours we safely launched the entire wing of 72 aircraft with pilots and maintenance technicians and secured the flight line should the storm intensify. The hurricane turned out to be very mild and there was no damage to the air base. However, that deployment was valuable in preparing us for another deployment that would occur only a couple of months later.

Soon after Anwar Sadat, President of Egypt, was assassinated in 1981, a major U.S. exercise was developed to deploy an Army brigade and a USAF A-10 squadron to the desert known as Cairo West Air Base. Our wing was selected to deploy an A-10 squadron with 4 special mission C-130s. The Army would deploy directly from the U.S. and parachute onto the target. Our A-10s were tasked to provide Close Air Support (CAS) for the airborne landing and on-ground operations. This exercise became the foundation of future long range airborne and close air support deployments, including Desert Shield/Storm.

We pre-position half of the pilots and maintenance people in the Azores and I headed that group. Our A-10s would deploy with KC-135 tankers from Myrtle Beach to the Azores. We were in the Azores to quick-turn the airplanes for the remainder of the trip to Egypt.

As we were preparing to receive the A-10s from Myrtle Beach, my boss on the KC-135 tanker that was fueling them reported that one of the A-10s could not transfer fuel from the external tanks into the airplane. It was a Very Big Problem. Without that external fuel, there was not enough fuel to get him to the Azores. The refueling tanker had departed thinking that all the A-10s were fully fueled and it did not have enough fuel to return to top off the problem A-10. I gathered our team together, we prayed that God would enable the external fuel to be normally transferred into the A-10. I radioed my boss and he reported that the fuel had just begun to transfer. All the airplanes landed with no further problems and that airplane didn't have a problem on subsequent flights. Again, God has answered prayers.

A tent city had been set up for us in Egypt. I chose not to bunk with the senior officers but to go to the tents reserved for the pilots. I wanted to get to know "my guys" better and I was still very new to the wing. My first wakeup was hearing morning Muslim prayers being blared outside the tent where I slept. The jolt of the prayers, being in a sleeping bag, and deep in REM sleep brought into the shock of reality of why and where we were.

We set up the airplanes for both static ground-based displays and live fire exercises with the Army. There was a large bombing range in the desert. Egypt had purchased many Soviet made vehicles and had placed them on the range to be used as targets for live weapons. Normally, A-10 pilots were restricted to firing at wooden targets on ranges in the U.S. Here it was a great thrill to finally fire the big 30mm gun against Soviet designed and built tanks and personnel carriers. It was clear that the A-10 could destroy the tanks and other equipment as would be repeatedly proven years later in Desert Storm.

A live fire demonstration was arranged with senior U.S. and Egyptian military officers attending in the stands near the staged targets. The Egyptian Air Force was to narrate the demonstration. Fortuitously, one of our squadron flight surgeons spoke Egyptian. He was translating the narration into English with the loud speakers blaring both the Egyptian and English versions. However, he was having trouble keeping up with the Egyptian narrator. One of the USAF generals grabbed me and shoved me up to the reviewing stand to do the English version. I protested that I knew absolutely nothing about what the Egyptian was saying. He replied that he didn't care and that I did know which airplanes were employing which weapons and for me to get busy providing English narration. I would watch as the A-10s, gunships, or F-16s began their attack then postulate what was going to happen. I was correct most of the time and the spectators seemed satisfied.

We had set up some 50-gallon barrels as targets for the A-10s to fly low and strafe with the 30mm gun. They would strafe one set then roll left or right to the other set. I had them turn toward the audience to further demonstrate the A-10s maneuverability, accuracy and destructive power. When the A-10s fired the 30mm gun, the noise and smoke were punctuated by the target barrels being thrown all over the place. As quickly as one A-10 came off the target, the next one was firing. It was a very impressive demonstration of Close Air Support.

The Egyptians were very friendly and invited us into their Soviet made SA-2 missile sites and explained how they would be employed. This was valuable intelligence for us since we anticipated flying against those types of anti-aircraft missiles in any future combat.

An interesting aside to the deployment occurred one evening at dinner. The Army Colonel that was directing the airborne side of the operation came over to our mess tent. As he walked to my table, I immediately recognized him as a colleague during our days at the Pentagon OJCS. We talked a minute, then we sat at another table and recalled out time at the Pentagon. During one of his special projects, he had come back to the office to ask me about the A-10 and how it could provide Close Air Support (CAS) to a ground operation. I recommended that an A-10 squadron could support the number of troops that he was planning. Now in Egypt, he explained that his Pentagon project was the study for the deployment we were on. Life often has a way for "what goes around, comes around." He had planned the Army deployment and I had added the A-10 CAS package. We were now each leading what we had designed years earlier. It is encouraging to see that paper exercises can be successfully executed.

Moreover, as mentioned earlier, the combined Army/A-10 close air support team was critical to the success of Desert Storm.

On my return home to Myrtle Beach, our family tried to get to the beach as often as possible. We told the boys that we didn't need to push too hard because we would be there for a couple of years or more. Our plan was that my boss would retire or move, and I would replace him. Later, we would learn that the boys would slip away from the house, cross the busy highway and enjoy the beach. Maybe they knew something that I didn't know.

The wing command section was especially friendly and professionally qualified. We worked well together, as evidenced by the successful hurricane and Egyptian deployments. The wives enjoyed each other's company. One morning as I walked to the car, there was a big sign over the entrance to our carport. I went back in the house and brought B.J. out to see, "Lordy, Lordy, B.J.'s 40." Her "friends" had been there early that morning to publicly wish her a happy birthday.

Good News and Bad News

Normally my boss would go to the afternoon "Stand Up Briefing" where the health of the wing was presented, and any issues addressed. We had been at Myrtle Beach less than a year when the Command Post called me and said that the Wing Commander had asked me to come to the briefing. After the briefings, he dismissed everyone but asked me to come to the table.

He began the conversation, "I have some good news, and some bad news." He explained that the good news was that I was being promoted to be the Deputy Commander of Operations, but the bad news was that it wouldn't be at Myrtle Beach. I was going to be assigned to England AFB, Louisiana.

Home for dinner, I began the conversation with the family in the same way, "We have good news and bad news." We weren't ready to move. Professionally I was doing well, and the family was enjoying Myrtle Beach. We had only been there a few months. The boys would be moving in the middle of the school year (again). Regardless, orders were orders and we began making plans to move (again).

The 23rd Tactical Fight Wing, England AFB (1982-1983)

The 23rd TFW was steeped in history as a successor to the 23rd Flying Tigers of WWII fame. It was based in the Louisiana homeland of General Claire Chenault and continued the tiger teeth on the nose of the A-10s as they had been painted on the P-40s in WWII.

I was proud to fly with the Flying Tigers

The Wing Commander, Jimmie Adams, and his wife welcomed us with open arms. They were a pleasure to work with and we continued to be friends after both he and I had left England AFB. He progressed quickly to become a 4-Star General. We would be stationed with them again later.

I was happy that I had met several pilots from England AFB during my initial A-10 training at Davis Monthan and thought that it would be a good start for me there.

Soon after arriving, I was selected to investigate an A-10 crash that occurred in an Air National Guard wing. I formed a team of the safety officer and pilot from our wing and we added a technical expert from Fairchild, the manufacturer of the A-10. Our investigation interviewed the pilot, the pilots in his formation, and people on the ground. We relied on experts that could look at the recovered flight displays and instruments and tell us the dynamic position of the airplane when it hit the ground. We determined that the crash was caused by a young pilot who overly aggressively maneuvered the airplane during the landing approach. He simply over shot the turn to final approach and pulled too hard trying to recover a poor situation and stalled the airplane in the famous "turn-to-final" phase. Fortunately, he ejected safely, and the airplane crashed on airport property with no significant damage to the surrounding area. We finished the investigation and I travelled to Langley AFB to brief the 4-star commander. He was satisfied that we had properly identified the cause and made the appropriate recommendations. Perhaps this investigation and report were the stepping stones to a later assignment.

The family was doing well in Louisiana. We bought a horse for Derek and the necessary truck and horse trailer, but Doug was feeling left out. Fortunately, the man who owned the feed store that we used offered to allow us to lease one of his horses, a Palomino that had one eye put out. We drafted an agreement and Doug contributed the fee of $1.00 in compliance with the provisions of the lease agreement. The boys got involved in horse riding and games and were enjoying their time in Louisiana. We also bought a water ski boat and made Doug the Captain responsible for keeping the boat ready to go on short notice. Derek had his 15th birthday which permitted him to get a driver's license. Our leisure time in Louisiana was punctuated by horse shows, fishing, and water skiing. We took one trip to New Orleans to show the boys where their parents had celebrated their honeymoon.

The wing leadership under Jimmie Adams was superb. I was the Director of Operations (DO). Ed Albritton was the Director of Maintenance (MA). When I arrived, Ed and I got together and decided there was no benefit in an argument between Operations and Maintenance. We worked any competing issues together for the common good of the combat capability of the wing. I had a sign in my office that said, "Have you hugged the MA today?" When we saw each other at the Officers Club, we would give each other a hug. He was a former college football player and I had to stand tall. Our intent was to publicly demonstrate that Operations and Maintenance were together. Our cooperative efforts were tested in an Operational Readiness Inspection (ORI) which we passed with flying colors. Soon our Wing Commander was promoted and reassigned. His replacement was not of the same caliber.

As was the case at Myrtle Beach, the wing commander called me to his office one day saying the four-star general commander of the Tactical Air Command wanted to interview me. I made a couple of trips to Langley AFB to meet him before finally getting the interview. Soon after the interview, I received orders to become the Director of Safety for the Tactical Air Command requiring a move to Virginia. I have wondered if it was my investigation of the A-10 crash that was the impetus for this new assignment. Regardless, after only 18 months in Louisiana we were moving to Virginia.

On the Road Yet Again, to Langley AFB, VA (1983-1985)

We were able to delay the move until the boys finished the school year. As previously mentioned, Derek got his driver's license at age 15, a couple of weeks before our move. With the household goods on the road, we loaded our horse, Baron, into his trailer and began another caravan. B.J. and Doug in the 280Z followed Derek, Baron, two Golden Retrievers and me in the truck and horse trailer.

I wanted our boys to get to know Dad's oldest brother, Ural. Uncle Ural agreed to allow us to stop at his house in North Carolina on our way to Virginia and they could help find a place for the horse. Great. Now we needed a place between Louisiana and North Carolina to stop where Baron could stretch his legs. We found a horse farm that allowed overnight boarding, called them, and they agreed. They were raising Saddlebred horses, huge and beautiful specimens. When Baron exited the trailer, he thought he had arrived in heaven. The next day it was almost impossible to get him back in the trailer to continue our trip. We learned another lesson. At our first rest stop along the interstate, we let Baron out of the trailer and Derek took him for a walk. Soon every kid in the area was running over to see Baron. Again, he didn't want to get back in the trailer. We decided that it wouldn't be necessary to let him out again until we were at the destination for the evening.

Arriving at Uncle Ural's house we asked where they were planning on Baron staying. He quickly replied, "In the garden." Their garden was fenced, and the produce was about finished. We led Baron into the garden, and he was set for the night. Aunt Polly met us the next morning laughing about being shocked when she looked out of her kitchen window and saw a horse looking back at her. Uncle Ural was true to my recollection of him. A couple of days of the boys hearing Uncle Ural's stories and learning how to whittle and we were loading Baron and continuing the trip to Virginia.

Derek had the opportunity to learn about driving on interstates and pulling a horse trailer at the age of 15 and only a couple of weeks of having a driver's license in his pocket. It all went well and was valuable experience as he became the chauffer of the Langley AFB Horse Club and hauled his horse and others to shows.

Crossing the draw bridge across the James River which had a grated roadbed, the tires on the truck and trailer began a noise and vibration that Baron had never known. Doug was following with Mom in the 280Z and yelled, "Mom, Baron is going to go to the bathroom." She saw the raised tail and hit the brakes to prevent Baron's download from being an upload on the front of her sports car. Doug's warning and her quick reaction prevented an immediate stop for a car wash. There was a Horse Club on base, and we had previously arranged to have a stall for Baron. He was settled before we were.

Arriving at Headquarters, Tactical Air Command, Langley AFB, VA

The base is located just outside of Hampton, VA and on the shores of the Chesapeake Bay. It was built before WWII and is beautiful with tree-lined streets, big houses and large buildings that house the Headquarters of the Tactical Air Command. Co-located are NASA test facilities, including a huge wind tunnel. NASA test is across the runway. The NASA facilities were instrumental in putting man in space and on the moon. Much of the *Hidden Numbers* movie was filmed where it happened, here at Langley AFB.

I would be one of only a few colonels that directly reported to the 4-Star commander. We were assigned one-half of one of the lovely, large duplex homes that was walking distance to work. The boys would go to the Hampton schools. However, we soon learned that there was an excellent Christian school just off the base. We decided the boys should continue their education in a Christian environment.

My job as Director of Safety was to establish safety policy and execute safety rules and regulations across the Tactical Air Command (TAC). TAC "owned" all the tactical fighters and their support bases across the Continental U.S. Its wartime mission was to provide fully trained pilots, maintenance technicians, and other personnel for the world-wide combined combat commands. Accordingly, it was one of the lead commands for the entire Air Force. I reported directly to the

4-Star that had interviewed me for the job. I was included in the staff meetings and deliberative meetings.

In my safety role, I oversaw the flight, ground, weapons, and nuclear safety aspects of the command. It was a very broad responsibility, from vehicles and airplanes to nuclear weapons storage. Safety is a core value of the Air Force and I had been involved from the airplane side from squadron and wing levels. However, the ground and weapons departments were new to me. I was extremely fortunate to have a career Chief Master Sergeant leading the ground safety program. He knew everything there was to know about it. And, he was very well connected to the ground safety people in the field operations. Weapons safety also was well covered. With those aspects being under excellent direction, I could concentrate on the flight safety side. It is impossible to eliminate all risks to safety. However, it is possible, even imperative, to manage and reduce the risks. For years we had used the phrase, "Fly Safe." I decided to change it to "Fly Smart" to emphasize that being smart will significantly contribute to flying safely. During my nearly three years there, the flight safety record was dramatically improved with the accident rate being cut by 25%. Ground and weapons safety enjoyed similar improvement. The USAF awarded our command the Flight Safety of the Year award each of the last two years of my assignment and I was asked to present our program to other USAF commands.

The commander allowed me to continue to fly the A-10 and directed that I visit all flying organizations and receive an "Executive Checkout" in the F-15 and F-16. I continued to fly the front seat of those airplanes every quarter or so for the next two years.

As we had at previous assignments, we immediately looked for a church. A good friend recommended Phoebus Baptist Church. We went there and quickly became members. We fell in love with the pastor, Brother Leonard Riley. We invited our next-door neighbors and started a Bible Study in our home with them and two or three other couples who lived on Langley AFB. Soon Phoebus Baptist moved from the small town of Phoebus closer to the base and we continued to attend there until we were reassigned a couple of years later. Our knowledge of the Bible and serving our Lord grew quickly and we made many great friends at church and in the Bible study. The boys were growing too. Derek became a "Shepherd" responsible for mentoring the younger boys in the church.

Sunday afternoons were rather lazy around our house. On one of them, our boys were messing with each other and getting louder and more boisterous with time. I yelled at Derek to get the racquetball equipment and that I was taking him to the gym. He got the balls and racquets, but not the safety glasses. After an appropriate warm up, I challenged him by beginning to serve. I was being uncommonly accurate in placing the serve in his left-handed corner where he could not get a good shot at it. After every successful serve, I would turn around and brag about it. I did that one too many times. He caught the next one and fired it hard back toward the front wall. However, my left eye was in the way. It struck me directly in the left eyeball and I fell to the ground. I knew I was hurt and asked him to join me in praying over my eye. We then got up and he drove us home.

Arriving there, the Command Surgeon was washing his car next door. We told what had happened, he looked at the eye and said, "Oh my, go the hospital now, I will meet you there." We grabbed B.J. and went directly to the base hospital. Within minutes of arriving, he was there accompanied by the hospital commander. The emergency room staff had already looked at me and decided I needed to be admitted to the hospital because blood was inside the lens. However, upon further consideration, the two senior doctors tore up the paper work explaining that if I was officially admitted to the hospital it would be reported to my boss, the four-star commander. He would not have been happy that his Chief of Safety had played racquetball with no safety glasses.

They sent me home with an eye patch and specific medicine to resolve the blood from behind the lens. I was told to lie down with my head elevated to permit the blood to slide to the lower part of the lens where it would not cause total vision problems. We called Brother Leonard and he came to the house. He laid his hand on me and prayed. He then got up to leave. I suggested there was no need to rush off. He responded that the Lord had told him to come and pray, not to stay and visit, and he left.

My sight returned after about a week of being quiet in bed, and I went back to work. As I walked through the flight safety department, all my fighter pilot flight safety guys were sitting at their desks. They didn't say a word. They kept looking down through the racquetball glasses they were wearing. They didn't need to say anything. They made their point. Do NOT play racquetball without safety glasses. I thought it was a good gesture and I greatly appreciated their pointed humor. Praise the Lord, there was no lasting damage to my eye, only to my ego.

Another Good News, Bad News, Good News Situation

After about a year and a half of my assignment at HQ TAC, our commander retired and was replaced by Jerry O'Malley, the general with whom I had worked at the Pentagon. He was now a four-star general on his way to become the Air Force Chief of Staff. We were excited to see the innovative ideas, improved relationships, and upward vector of the command. And he seemed glad to see me. I met with him several times. While he made no promises about my future, things were looking up for us.

Sadly, about six months after his arrival, he and his wife were voluntarily going to speak to a Boy Scout meeting in Pennsylvania and were flying there in a USAF executive transport airplane. Upon landing the brakes failed and the airplane overran the runway and slid down a very steep cliff. Everyone on board died in the ensuing fire. B.J. and I were personally devastated to lose such a wonderful couple and consummate general officer. His untimely death dramatically changed the direction of the USAF, and not for the better. We attended his funeral and burial at the Arlington National Cemetery.

General O'Malley was replaced by another excellent general officer. However, he did not know me. Consequently, when reassignment time came, I was down the priority list and the call came to offer me to be the USAF deputy in Egypt. I quickly made the decision to not accept the assignment and was told I had seven days to either accept the assignment or retire. My first call was to B.J. to pray about this offer. Next, I called the three-star deputy commander and asked to see him. He agreed to see me. I put on my Class A uniform and walked over to his office. Saluting him, he said, "Sit down, I know why you are here." I explained my reasons for rejecting the assignment: 1) I wanted to be a wing commander and I would be out of the career time window when I returned from Egypt, 2) I had boys in high school, and 3) As he knew, as Born-Again Christian I asked the Lord if this was for me to serve him there, and did not get a positive response. He picked up the intercom to the senior officer assignments and told him to put my assignment on hold.

A month or so later I received the good news that I was being assigned to be the Wing Commander of the 24th Composite Air Wing at Howard AFB, Panama. Again, my first call was to B.J., but this time with good news.

Preparing for Panama

We immediately had some decisions to make. Both boys were doing well in school and this would be a mid-year move for them. Derek was a Senior and active in school. Our next-door neighbor was an AF Academy grad, was in our church, in our home Bible Study, and their family was very close to our family. In fact, their son and Derek were the same age, in the same class, the same soccer team, and good friends. They offered that Derek could live with them and graduate from high school, then he could move to Panama to join us.

Initially, that sounded like a promising idea to all of us. However, after giving it considerable thought, Derek came into our bedroom where we were reading while lying on the bed. He jumped onto the bed between us and we three discussed it. He had decided that he would like to come with us and graduate in Panama. We were happy with his decision.

We began packing household goods, selling a car, shipping B.J.'s 280Z, and arranging for our two Golden Retrievers to travel on the commercial flight with us to Panama. Unfortunately, there is a quarantine for live animals coming into Panama. The military had a veterinarian facility that would keep the dogs for the two-month isolation. We visited them several times, but each time we left with sadness that they were put back into the kennels until the quarantine period was over.

Chapter 14: A Goal Met: Wing and Air Division Commander in Panama

The 24th Composite Air Wing, Panama (1985-1988)

I asked that the change of command be on December 3rd, 1985 because it would be B.J.'s birthday and a special event for both of us. They agreed, and we took over from a very highly qualified colonel that I had met at previous activities. He was well liked and was gracious in his introductory remarks at our change of command.

It is unfortunate that civilian organizations have not copied the Change of Command Ceremony. It is a well-established process in the military. The night before, there is a party for the outgoing commander during which everyone can express their goodbyes and kind words. The next morning the organization assembles with pomp and ceremony during which the outgoing commander relinquishes command to his senior then that senior assigns it to the new commander. Each of these officers has the opportunity to make a few comments. Following the formal ceremony there is a reception at the officers' club during which everyone can welcome the new commander and his wife.

Our ceremony was extremely well done. The 12th Air Force Commander, a 3-star general, officiated. He was a brilliant officer, held a PhD, and was well respected both as a senior leader and pilot. He was very kind in his remarks and in his discussions with me following the ceremony. The wing had prepared a well-orchestrated reception following the ceremony. Both B.J. and I were honored and excited to begin this new chapter in our lives. I thanked the wing and staff for the professional change of command ceremony and reception.

Howard AFB with the Pacific Ocean in the background

The wing was in a state of transition as was Panama. The currently assigned airplanes were older O-2As, a military version of the Cessna 337. The O-2s had been widely used in Vietnam by forward air controllers to locate and attack the enemy. That was their mission in Panama, but with faster attack airplanes, the O-2s were no longer effective. Consequently, the OA-37 was coming to replace them. The OA-37 was a modified T-37 jet with larger engines, external fuel tanks, 7.62mm mini-Gatling Gun, and provisions to carry and deliver bombs and rockets. More capable than the O-2, the OA-37 could not only locate the enemy but also could deliver ordnance to destroy it. In addition, the OA-37 could be refueled in flight by using the probe on the airplane to engage a drogue from a KC-135 or KC-10 aircraft thus dramatically extending its operational range. We completed the transition more than a month early and well under budget.

Wing transitioned to the OA-37 a month early and below budget.

The pilots in the wing were trained Forward Air Controllers (FACs) who would be the eyes of the attacking aircraft to identify enemy targets and provide precise direction for the attack. We had vehicles with both airborne and Army radios to facilitate communication between the ground and air forces. Moreover, several of our FACs were jumped qualified and could parachute with the Army Airborne forces directly to the fight. The forward controllers could be on the ground in command vehicles or in the air in the OA-37.

The wing had dual reporting responsibilities. In peacetime I reported to the Commander, 12th Air Force, the three-star general located in Austin, Texas. Should there be a war commitment, the wing could transfer operational control to the United States Southern Command which was commanded by an Army four-star general.

Panama was in the transition from domination from the United States due to the US "owning" the Panama Canal Zone, a strip of land that was several miles wide and extending from the Pacific to the

Atlantic Oceans. However, President Jimmy Carter had negotiated a new treaty that would return all the Canal Zone and the U.S. military bases to the Panamanians on January 1st, 2000. Earlier I mentioned that while on the OJCS at the Pentagon, I had been associated with the military input to that treaty. Now, I was implementing it.

It is very interesting that all the details of the treaty were not well known by Congressional Leaders who should have known, and who voted for treaty ratification. Within a couple of weeks of my taking command, then Senator Strom Thurman visited on his way to spend the Christmas holidays with a former Panamanian ambassador to the U.S. at his home on Contedora Island, the same island that hosted the Shah of Iran when he was disposed. Senator Thurman arrived on a USAF transport aircraft that was making a scheduled trip to Panama. He would transfer to a small aircraft that could land on Contedora. While they were processing his passport and we waited on the small aircraft, I drove him around the base, pointing out the view to the Canal, the Pacific, and the entire base. As we sat on the large flight line with only a few air operations on a warm Sunday afternoon just before Christmas, he said in his best South Carolina drawl, "Now tell me Colonel, does all this transfer to the Panamanians in 2000?" I replied, "Yes sir, it does." He lowered his head and said, "That damn Jimmy Carter." It was obvious that the senior senator on the Armed Services Committee didn't know that the treaty required that all the U.S. Army, Navy and Air Force bases would transfer to Panama.

An embarrassing thing happened within days of taking command. I was invited by the Senior Enlisted Advisor to have Christmas lunch in the mess hall with the troops and to bring the family. As we exited the line, the cashier told me what the charge would be. I didn't have enough money with me and B.J. had not brought her purse. After explaining, the Chief paid my bill. He was a fantastic Chief Master Sergeant who had taken advantage of the educational benefits of the Air Force and had worked his way through college to obtain a PhD. Moreover, he was at home with the troops and was a valued and trusted advisor to me. Obviously, we went home, found enough money and quickly paid him back, but the chagrin was established.

I had completed training in the OA-37 while still in the U.S. I flew one sortie with an Instructor Pilot as a local checkout. My other duties didn't permit me a lot of time to fly. However, I tried to fly every week. I also wanted to fly the O-2A while they were still available and asked an instructor to go with me. I quickly qualified in all the weapons delivery methods in both aircraft. Since the OA-37 had two seats, a second person could fly. Often, the second person was an instructor pilot. In some instances, a junior pilot would fly with me just to get more flying time, get to know me and me him, and I could transfer some of the skills that I had learned over time to him.

I also wanted to introduce as many of my staff as possible to the joys and strategies of our mission and started the Incentive Flight Program. We flew deserving non-pilot personnel who had demonstrated excellence in their jobs. The flights were the missions that were scheduled for that day. Consequently, it created no additional workload for maintenance or any other support activity. I personally flew several, including some of the women on my staff who were consummate professionals in various responsibilities throughout the wing. We fired rockets, shot the gun, and dropped the practice bombs. I think the Public Affairs Officer was the only one that experienced a little stomach upset. After flying five of them, they reported to my office in their dress uniforms and presented me the first ever "Order of the Pink Garter" for having flown each of them. I was honored.

B.J. quickly assumed her "duties" as the commander's wife. While there are no official responsibilities, there are the unwritten, sometimes verbal, directions of her role. She quickly became very involved with the new baby programs. Many new babies were coming into the world in young marriages a long way from family support. She established a network that came along side new mothers, provided layette bundles, and supported new moms. She was very involved with both the Officers Wives Club and the Enlisted Wives Club. These clubs provided the social structure that was essential to helping wives in an international environment. They were very involved in charitable activities both on and off base. Of course, we also immediately joined the chapel and started a Bible study.

The boys enrolled in the Panama Canal Zone schools which had been established when the canal was being built and were operated under the Department of Defense school programs. Derek was a senior and had to jump into the school in the middle of the year. Doug was in Middle School. Their transition was fairly smooth as they made new friends and became academically established in the schools. Derek decided he would play football for the first time and Doug went on with soccer. Derek graduated from Balboa High School and entered Panama Canal College. His work there transferred to Texas A&M a year later. Doug was equally successful and moved up the Middle School grades.

The boys enjoyed Panama, mainly because of the extracurricular activities. Outdoor sports dominated. The boys and I went through the PADI deep sea diving classes and received our certifications that are still valid. Derek was old enough to go through the SCUBA training alone. However, Doug had to wait to attend with me which was a great benefit to me. I had never been a good swimmer, but Doug had been on swim teams. Toward the end of the course, we had to deposit all our gear on the bottom of the pool, surface, then swim down to retrieve and put it on. As I made the attempt, I couldn't quite reach the regulator and exhaled to reduce buoyancy. But as I grabbed the mouthpiece, it was filled with water and I couldn't inhale. As I fought to the surface I was totally out of breath. The instructor grabbed me to make sure I wouldn't drown, then told me I couldn't graduate unless I could perform the maneuver. I dove again. Approaching the gear, I felt a hand grab me, then insert the mouthpiece into my mouth. Now with plenty of air I could don the remaining equipment. Swimming to the surface I saw Doug sitting on the edge of the pool with a big smile. He had dived into the pool, swum underwater, grabbed the equipment and me, and ensured that I would graduate so that he could get his certification. Sometimes, sons must help their dads. On the open water graduation dive, Doug, I and three other men were in a small boat off the shore of Panama. A pod of dolphins came swimming by, and the dive master said we could jump overboard and swim with them. They were very tame and swam right to us. There was one small baby with its mother, and she allowed Doug to reach out and touch her. Other dive trips were equally enjoyable. Derek's graduation celebration was a special dive trip to Curaçao with one of his classmates and family.

The wing was responsible for a very nice golf course and the boys and I took advantage as often as we could. When I went to the course, the caddies and staff always asked where the boys were. There was a standing tee time for 8:00 every Saturday morning for me and the top three of my senior staff. It was a great informal time for us to get to know each other. We played quickly, and the course management soon learned to block the tee time in front of us because we would overrun them if they played slowly.

We had a short-notice visitor. Vice President Bush (later to become the 41st President and play a major role in Panama) was in Ecuador inspecting earthquake damage. His airplane had to refuel at Howard AFB on its return to Washington. I received permission for our family and our vice commander's family to come to the flight line to meet him. He was most gracious and arranged for the two families to have pictures with him in front of his airplane. I had the distinct honor to spend nearly two hours alone with him. I showed him some airplanes on the flight line. Walking back to the office he asked me if I had met General Noriega. I told him that I had. He then asked what I thought of him. I replied that he was "evil" and explained that Noriega was involved in every vice of money laundering, prostitution, drugs, and assassination of opponents. The Army commander's wife once told me after sitting beside General Noriega at a Christmas party that, "He reeks of death."

Vice President Bush and Our Family in Panama

When I first arrived in Panama and became the Wing Commander, there was an Air Force Major General living on Albrook AFB, the other base assigned to our wing and me. He commanded the USAF Southern Air Division (USAFSO), also reporting to 12th Air Force. He had a second responsibility as Vice Commander of the U.S. Southern Command. He had a small staff of USAF officers who were experts in Latin American Affairs. They had oversight of USAF aid going throughout Latin America. In addition, they represented the USAF in several Latin American military organizations and exercises.

I also had representational responsibilities with other Latin American nations. In that role, Noriega made me an honorary Panamanian Air

Force Pilot and awarded me Panamanian AF pilot wings. I travelled extensively throughout Latin America.

One of my units was the USAF Latin American Air Force Academy. It was the school for Latin American air force officers and enlisted to teach everything from maintaining vintage airplanes still be being flown by some Latin American countries to pilot training. When I arrived, it was commanded by a USAF Academy graduate who had extensive Latin American experience and was fluent in Spanish. I was totally dependent upon him to run the Academy. When he was about to be reassigned, I was very concerned about finding another equally qualified commander. Polling the network, I found there was a similarly qualified colonel, also an Air Force Academy graduate and fluent in Spanish, in Washington, DC who was about to retire. I called Gene Davis and persuaded him to withdraw his retirement and come to Panama. We were extremely blessed to have two superbly qualified men in that critical position. Both remain friends. Gene became my assistant in a civilian activity after we both had retired. More about that later.

About half-way through my assignment, the Air Force decided to combine USAFSO's Latin American Affairs Division under the 24th Wing and my command. When the former commander left, he did not assign his responsibilities to me or have a change of command for me. I had to call my boss in Texas who then directed me to write a letter assigning that responsibility to myself. He was replaced by another USAF two-star general whose singular responsibility was Vice Commander of the U.S. Southern Command. He lived at Albrook AFB and continued to expect me to provide support even though it was the responsibility of the Army to do so. I had known him for several years when we were in different capacities. However, the previous harmonious relationship did not continue in Panama.

Tensions with General Noriega Increased:

As mentioned earlier, the dual reporting arrangement is standard for air wings stationed overseas. However, it was unique to the 12th Air Force during peacetime. Unfortunately, the command relationships became muddied when General Noriega increased tensions between his government and the U.S. military. He threatened the U.S. Forces and civilian personnel living in Panama several times. He held up Christmas shipments that included toys for our kids in the Port of Colon, pulled a loaded train across the tracks preventing the school buses from leaving the Middle School, and he stationed troops around the various bases seemingly to test our readiness and security.

The staff and I were in a conference meeting to discuss various options should Noriega directly harass our base. The secretary interrupted the meeting to say I had a call from our younger son, Doug, a student in the Middle School. The family know that they could call anytime and if they insisted, I would take the call regardless of what I was doing. Both Doug and the Secretary confirmed I needed to take the call. He whispered that he was sorry to interrupt but that his Principal was standing beside him and had asked him to call me to get more information about how they were going to safely evacuate the kids. I assured Doug (and the Principal) that the train would soon be moving and that seemed to satisfy both. I knew that if the Panamanians didn't move it, the Army would. Soon we received a report that the train was moving, and the kids were safely on their buses headed home.

Howard Air Force Base was our main base with operational runway and airplanes, including a detachment of Army personnel and helicopters. It had two major security flaws. The first was a Panamanian highway that ran through the middle of the base including both the front and rear gates. The road serviced a small coastal town a couple of miles outside the base. We could not close the road without serious challenges to both the people who depended upon it and the Panamanian Government. The other security flaw was the jungle which immediately border the back side of the base. Any manner of problems could have been launched from the jungle into the base. Periodically there would be announcements in the newspaper that a demonstration would be held at our main gate. Our primary concern was that the demonstrators would get on a bus that routinely transited the base on the public highway, then jump off the bus when it stopped near one of our buildings or flight line with the demonstrators running through the base. When I presented this to my three-star boss, he said, "If they run through the housing areas or base, shoot them." I questioned him, and he repeated what he had said. I immediately went into my vice commander's office and repeated what the general had said and wrote it down should a contingency arise. While I think he was exaggerating for effect, I was not going to shoot a demonstrator unless they became violent and presented a clear and present danger to our people.

As the tensions from Noriega escalated, the U.S. Southern Command general began planning for various scenarios and contingencies. He asked me to provide a senior officer as the Air Component representative. While I probably should have taken that role, I wanted to be in command of the air wing should combat become necessary. Consequently, I appointed my vice commander to that role. Under a very limited scenario where combat could occur, and the USAF assets came under the unified command structure of the Southern Air Division, I would have been subordinate to the 4-star and to my vice commander. While that is a strange relationship, my vice commander and I clearly understood the relationship and we would make it happen.

The only serious threat to our base came one afternoon. I was jogging and heard a loud explosion from the direction of our ammunition storage area. I had my command radio (commonly called The Brick) and called the command post. Of course, they couldn't hear it from inside their building. I was concerned that the Panamanian Army had detonated a claymore mine, rocket or some other device. It created enough apprehension within the Army unit on the base that they placed a combat unit between our base and the jungle to protect their assets which were in that area, also shielding our base. That evening the Army one-star commander came to my command post. He and I walked the perimeter together to ensure the troops weren't trigger happy and that any Panamanian forces could see our readiness. By early morning, the threat was gone, and we recalled the troops from the defensive lines.

For the next 18 months or so, Noriega continued to harass Americans, both military and civilian. During this time the United States made every attempt to persuade him to retire and leave Panama. There were persistent rumors, both in Panama and the U.S., that offers of millions of dollars and a plush retirement in a friendly country were repeatedly rebuffed. Should he decide he would like to leave, a C-141 cargo aircraft was positioned at our base to facilitate his departure. Unfortunately, he was not leaving.

The wing operated very efficiently and effectively. We transitioned from the propeller-driven O-2A to the jet OA-37 ahead of schedule and below budget. Pilots, maintenance technicians and support personnel became very proficient and were declared Combat Ready ahead of schedule. Because I believe that leaders should lead, I had the operations team put me on the combat roster for one day even though I could not be officially counted in the readiness report. But it made the statement to the troops that I was ready.

Each Air Force wing receives a no-notice Operational Readiness Inspection every couple of years. Ours came nearly two years into my command and the inspection went well. I was very happy with the wing, its people and their performance. The wing made several deployments to Latin American countries to demonstrate USAF Air Power and work with the host country to improve its readiness. The Latin American Air Force Academy added pilot training to its curriculum, and we trained many pilots with our Spanish speaking instructor pilots. The tactical squadron commander had come directly from the F-16 and was very skilled in bringing the newest and best techniques and maneuvers to the operation. In the process of flying the OA-37s we could set a personal record for the time for a transcontinental flight from the Atlantic to the Pacific (or reverse the directions). My best time for a transcontinental flight was about 12 minutes.

Of course, there were disappointments along the way. One of our young pilots had an on-board fire soon after takeoff. He wisely flew out over the ocean at the end of our runway. He ejected with no injuries and was picked up by a fisherman and brought to shore. The Accident Board found that a line had ruptured and caused the fire. We inspected the other airplanes and found no problems.

My personal disappointment was in my relationship with my three-star commander. He was known as a guy who was hard to get along with, and while I am okay with highly demanding bosses, he was both unreasonable and demeaning. He verbally berated anyone who was not a fighter pilot, and our wing was a not a classic fighter wing. Moreover, I had C-130 aircraft temporarily assigned and he was downright mean to them. He really liked B.J. though and wrote her a thank you letter after she had prepared him a bean soup lunch, calling her a "World Class Wife of a Wing Commander." I totally agree with him. However, that seemed to be the only thing upon which we could agree.

We had invited a four-star general who had been our wing commander at England AFB and whom we had stayed in contact to visit us. He and his wife arrived, and we treated them to a great few days. Our Panamanian friend took them on his yacht for a short cruise and snorkeling trip. We also hosted a dinner with our senior staff. He asked me if I would like to be reassigned to a larger fighter wing. I considered that the boys had moved the year before and were now doing well and respectfully declined. Over the years it became clear that he was offering me the bigger wing to promote me to brigadier general and choosing not to move prevented that from happening. Moreover, not taking the new job left me under the old boss who would never promote me. Consequently, I would remain a colonel.

Official and Unofficial Representational Responsibilities

As the commander of the USAF Southern Air Division, I was asked to represent the Air Force in many diplomatic and social events. I was often included in activities outside of Panama. One trip was to Chile to meet with the Commander of the Chilean Air Force. Interestingly, the president came for dinner. I regularly attended meetings with the commanders of the air forces of Honduras, Guatemala, and El Salvador. These meetings were important in the days of the revolution in Nicaragua. In Panama, B.J. and attended social events with the U.S. Embassy, Army and Navy.

We were included in many off-base, Panamanian social activities. We were invited to a special gathering in the country where the local dignitaries were hosting a luncheon and party of the Miss Universe Pageant Competitors. The pageant was being held in Panama City. Miss USA walked up to Doug and said he was so handsome and began asking him questions. He was embarrassed but loved every minute of it. The owner of the ranch invited Doug to spend the summer working at his coffee ranch in the mountains. Given the tense situation in Panama and the remoteness of the ranch, we weren't ready to let Doug do that. It is unfortunate that he couldn't. He would have a had good time and returned fluent in Spanish.

I was asked to join a couple of the hosts at the back of the house. When we arrived, there were several men sitting in a circle in the shade. I was introduced, and the questions began. When are you Americans going to get rid of Noriega? Do you have bombs on those airplanes? Give me one and I will take care of "our" problem. Obviously, I would not participate in the discussion. I was respectful but quietly returned to the main party. It was obvious that they were tired of Noriega's dictatorship and were powerless to do anything about it. A couple of years later the U.S. did remove him.

About two and a half years into the command, the boss called and told me it was time for me to move. He offered two positions that I didn't want. I asked if he would assign me to 12th Air Force staff at

Bergstrom AFB, TX. I explained that the command could use my Latin American experience, our son was at Texas A&M, and we would like to get to Texas. Even though we had a very rocky relationship, he was kind and said he would honor that request. I have been very appreciative that he was gracious to assign us to Texas where we have been for the past thirty years, except for a couple of years in Florida and Virginia.

The change of command was scheduled, and I would be replaced by one of my Academy classmates. I had known him at The Academy, but we had not spent much time together in the Air Force. The wing was very kind to B.J. and me. They hosted several going away parties during which we were honored.

With no notice, the wives surprised B.J. in a dilapidated "Chiva Bus" that is popular in Panama. They were dressed in formal attire complete with white gloves and champagne when they arrived at our house to pick up B.J. As they drove around town, they could look through the holes in the floor to the highway below. Of course, the afternoon rains came, and water splashed through the floor, but they didn't care. They were having fun.

Chiva Bus

One of the parties was a surprise mobile feast, starting at one house and progressing to others led by a mariachi band. It was a spectacle in the execution, but we were immensely honored that they had gone to so much trouble to arrange the homes, food, and band as both a tribute and farewell to us.

We spent our last night in Panama with our Panamanian friends that had hosted the general and us on their yacht. They had been very kind at other times as well. After dinner, Doug learned that the grandfather of the family had been involved in Panamanian politics. Doug sat with him for more than an hour inquiring of the political intrigue of General Torrijos and General Noriega and the way that Noriega became Torrijos' successor.

The next day we boarded American Airlines flight to Miami to return to the United States and the next assignment at Bergstrom AFB, Texas. I was sad to leave the command and Panama. However, we always looked forward with great anticipation to what plan God had for us. We knew our Air Force days were coming to an end. We also knew that there would be many more great opportunities ahead.

Chapter 15: Turning Final, Retirement is Approaching

12th Air Force Headquarters, Bergstrom AFB, Austin, Texas (1988-1990)

About the time we arrived in Austin, the three-star general whom had been my boss when I was in Panama was reassigned and another three-star whom I had known replaced him. Clearly, this was a retirement assignment for me. Regardless, I jumped in with both feet to work toward developing plans for war and for the peaceful operation of the command.

Since 12th AF was the parent command of my old wing in Panama, I was able to add local information to the contingency plans. Noriega was still there, and the tense situation would soon escalate. A group of young USAF men were officially visiting Howard AFB but decided to go into Panama City for dinner. While that was quite fine, and we often shopped and dined there, they went into a bad part of town. They came upon a road block and decided that they didn't have to stop there. Tragically, a Panamanian soldier or police officer fired, striking one of them and he died. Clearly, the United States would not allow that to go unnoticed and without repercussion. President George H. W. Bush would retaliate over Christmas 1989 using some of the plans and targets that I had worked when I was in Panama and at 12th AF. The wing was involved in both active combat and in supporting the U.S. forces that deployed there. The result was that Noriega was forced to take refuge in the Catholic priest's home which our military would not attack. However, he ultimately surrendered and was taken to Miami for trial and imprisonment. Noriega had been given multiple opportunities to leave Panama with his family, money, and a safe retirement. His refusal cost both U.S. and Panamanian lives and treasure. Since his departure, Panama has prospered and flourished under a democratic government that has reduced crime and corruption. The patriots that I met a couple of years earlier finally achieved the results they desired.

Other duties at 12th AF included moving the headquarters to Davis-Monthan AFB, Arizona and preparing Bergstrom to be turned over to the city of Austin for development into what would become Austin-Bergstrom International Airport. Interestingly, the headquarters building would become a hotel. For a time, if you had worked in that building, you could make a reservation with the hotel to spend the night and ask for your old office to be your hotel room. Later a second runway was built on the east side of the complex. The north end of that runway terminated where our house had stood.

Another project was the relocation of the Latin American Air Forces Academy from Albrook AFB, Panama to Homestead AFB, FL. I was very involved in that move since the Academy had reported to me. I had recruited Gene Davis to withdraw his retirement to command the Academy and he was exactly the right guy to prepare and make the move. It was a huge project to pack up all the equipment and move the people. But he made it happen.

Decision Time: Air Force or Retirement

There is a milestone for military colonels contemplating retirement. At the 26-year point, a significant pay raise occurs. As I approached that point, I was ready to leave my love of the USAF to pursue other challenges. B.J. and I discussed it and we decided to retire, but we had many reservations. In praying for divine guidance, she was led to Jeremiah 29:11, "*For I know the plans I have for you, declares the Lord, plans to prosper you and not to harm you, to give you a hope and a future*" (NIV). She immediately called from home to me in the office, and that verse became our strength and affirmation to retire.

I began talking with civilian friends about potential job opportunities. Several said they would like to hire me or recommend me to their friends. I interviewed with the upstart Dell Corporation but didn't have the necessary computer background. I also interviewed with a holding company, the president was in my Sunday School class. He explained that while he could use my leadership, he could hire a new accounting major from the University of Texas for a lower salary and could train him/her to stay with the company for many years. Similar answers came from other interviews.

There was no definitive offer until I received a call from the Vice President of DynCorp Aircraft Services. They were considering bidding on a major project to operate the U.S. Department of State air assets committed to the drug fight in Latin America. One of their employees who had worked for me in Panama had highly recommended me. The VP arranged to come to Austin for dinner with his wife, B.J. and me. I thought the interview went well. Later, I received a call from the corporate VP for Operations asking if I would be in Washington. As it turned out, I was on a business trip the next week and we scheduled breakfast. Unknown to me, he had checked me out with one of their corporate board members who was my AF Academy classmate and he had highly recommended me. I got the job.

There was a retirement ceremony in front of the headquarters in Austin for me and for my friend who had been the first commander of the Latin American Air Force Academy when we arrived in Panama. I was honored to share the stage with him. After appropriate speeches and the formal presentation of retirement orders and awards we adjourned to the Officer's Club for a short reception where we could say goodbyes to many friends and colleagues. Our older son, Derek, was in college, but B.J. and Doug were at the ceremony and reception. In a large sense, they also were retiring. B.J. had been the wind beneath my wings from the Academy and through the joys and tribulations of 26 years in the Air Force. The boys were born into the Air Force and had served faithfully in very demanding moves in the middle of school, making new friends, and seeing both the good and not so good aspects of military life.

I officially retired on July 1, 1990. Both B.J. and I received certificates thanking us for our service and I was awarded another Legion of Merit.

After the Retirement Ceremony, we were treated to a reception at the Officers' Club at Bergstrom AFB, TX.

We moved into a small house in Austin and enjoyed a relaxing Independence Day weekend before I reported to my new job at DynCorp in Fort Worth, Texas.

Derek From Panama to Texas A&M and Beyond (1987-1991)

Derek headed off to college at Texas A&M after attending one year at Panama Canal College. We flew the whole family to Texas and began the in-processing efforts. The first evening he went to a "mixer" of transferring students and met a young man from Tyler, Texas. Interestingly, the next morning as we were walking to a session, this guy and his dad joined with us. We chatted as we entered the building and decided to sit together. After the session, we told them that we were going to the student housing office to find an apartment. As we walked into that office, they walked in immediately after us. We began going through the cards together and the boys began talking with each other about rooming together. I sent them off to another room to decide. They returned saying they would like to share an apartment and we parents agreed. We had talked with the dad and learned that they were Born Again Christians and were very active in their church. We left together to find them an apartment. This casual meeting of two boys transferring into Texas A&M was a Divine Appointment that became a lifetime friendship.

Derek had some time before classes started and we left him with very dear friends, Glenn and Barbara Jones. We had known them throughout our USAF careers, Glenn was an Aggie grad, and they lived in Grapevine, Texas. Glenn got Derek a job at the Hunt Ranch for the summer prior to entering A&M. They were very gracious to Derek. We were in Panama and were seriously restricted in how we could help him. They were surrogate parents and helped him transition to being away from home and entering Texas A&M.

B.J., Doug and I returned to Texas to get Derek started at A&M. We had an agreement that we wouldn't cry or get all emotional about leaving our oldest and returning to Panama. However, as I was driving off campus, I looked in the mirror to see Doug in the corner of the back seat beginning to cry. That did it. B.J. and I joined him in the sadness.

With God, there are no accidents. Meeting Brian Jacobe and his dad in the mass of people on orientation day at Texas A&M was no accident. Rather, it was a God-ordained meeting that would remain important today. Since we were in Panama, Brian invited Derek to go home to Tyler, Texas with him on weekends. Derek became very involved in their church and met a young lady that would capture his heart.

After our assignment in Panama was complete, we returned to the United States and set out on an extensive road trip. Again, we bought a car from the Exchange Service and picked it up in Miami. B.J., Doug and I began the trip from Miami to Texas. Derek joined us in Indiana when we stopped to meet the Watson family. Our next stop was in Colorado to visit the Douglas family. We wound up in Texas. However, before we started out with the new assignment, Derek insisted we go to Tyler to meet Kelly Hunnicutt and her family. We enjoyed a couple of days visiting them and their church and could see that Derek and Kelly were making plans for marriage.

Brian Jacobe graduated at Christmas 1990 and would be moving from the apartment he and Derek had shared for three years. Derek came to us with a plan for another roommate. We had met Kelly and her family several times over the previous couple of years. Derek explained that he thought he and Kelly should get married during Christmas break and live in the apartment while he finished his final semester at A&M. We agreed, and the respective mothers began the wedding preparations. They were married in the church where they met, with the reception following in the Fellowship Hall. It was a lovely wedding and they were off on a honeymoon then to A&M. More about them in later chapters.

Mr. & Mrs. Derek and Kelly Watson

Doug and Austin (1988-1991)

When we arrived in Austin, the Austin school system for kids living on Bergstrom AFB and the surrounding neighborhoods was not very good and had discipline problems. We learned that Hyde Park Baptist Church had a school that enjoyed a good reputation. We joined the church and Doug began his Sophomore year at the school. Mom had to drive him from the base to the school in North Austin. When school started, we found there were a couple more boys of Doug's age that lived close to us and a car pool was formed. Doug joined the football team and enjoyed going to that school. However, the school in Panama was not as advanced and did not prepare him well. Yet, he overcame the challenges in both academics and football.

To his great embarrassment and my eternal chagrin, we purchased him a vehicle, not a super truck or car, but an old Honda Civic. We delivered it to school and his football teammates came out to see it. One look and they went back in to school. The affluent kids were not impressed. There were advantages to this old, little car. We could pay cash, he could now drive to school, and the car was a stick shift. About a year later we did trade it for a more respectable vehicle.

When I retired, we moved into Northwest Austin and Doug transferred to Anderson High School and graduated a year later. He attended summer school there and did very well. He was on the football team and quickly became active in this his third high school.

Chapter 16: Beyond the Air Force: Life in Corporate America

DynCorp, Fort Worth, Texas (1990-1991)

DynCorp was a very large company that provided world-wide maintenance services to the U.S. government. They were extremely well qualified to work on both aircraft and ground vehicles, primarily depending on employees who had previous government experience. The aviation services company in Fort Worth had a list of several thousand fully qualified technicians. The U.S. government would negotiate for DynCorp to provide highly skilled workers anywhere in the world, often on very short notice. Work could vary from repairing aircraft in a remote location to working on Navy ships and Army vehicles.

I was recruited to head the team that was developing a proposal to operate and maintain over 60 aircraft and helicopters fighting the drug war in several Latin American countries. The U.S. Department of State had issued a "Request for Proposal" for companies to develop pricing, schedule, procedures, and details to operate its counter-drug air unit. The current contractor was not doing well, and the unit would be moved from Miami-Opa Locka Airport, Florida to Patrick AFB, Florida. Our proposal team consisted of about six experts in proposal development and pricing and we were supported by others in Fort Worth and corporate headquarters. My job was to bring the people and their skills into a cohesive, winning team that would write the proposal to the Department of State. Frankly, I knew nothing about writing proposals. But I did know how to build teams and use the team's individual and collective experiences and knowledge to produce the best result.

DynCorp treated me quite well. They set up a corporate apartment near the office. I would drive from Austin early on Monday, stay in the apartment and work until Friday afternoon, then drive back home to B.J. and Doug in Austin. While I missed the family and they missed me, the apartment and 2-hour drive made it doable. When necessary, I could drive home one evening and back the next morning. The apartment was a two-bedroom unit that I would share with other guys who were working on my project.

Most of the team was assembled when I arrived. They had begun work and brought me into the project. They were very experienced in both DynCorp field operations and in the development and execution of government contracts. They carried the major duties and I was able to contribute from my experience as a wing commander and pilot in Latin America. The man who recommended me was my subject matter expert and go-to guy for details about DynCorp and contracting. As others were added to the team, I was quick to identify those that could be used in the negotiations with State and could be on the execution team if we won. The senior leadership in Fort Worth was especially helpful. They guided all of us toward a succinct proposal of how we would operate the contract and they developed pricing models based on their extensive experience on similar government contracts. In the days before word processors, the typists were extremely accurate, and the editors could turn technical-speak into sentences that evaluators could understand.

As we were busy writing, Iraq invaded Kuwait. The Kuwaiti Air Force flew their A-7 aircraft one mission against the attackers then landed in Saudi Arabia. One of the guys on my team had contacts with another government agency who called and asked if we could support the Free Kuwaiti Air Force that was exiled in Saudi Arabia. We immediately said yes then began looking at what could be done. Calling on the larger DynCorp capabilities, we quickly developed a plan and team to go to Saudi Arabia and serve as maintenance and support personnel for the Free Kuwait Air Force. We shipped them everything from uniforms and supplies to bombs and bullets. This small group grew into a separate division which still exists at DynCorp.

We contracted with major cargo airlines to pick up supplies and fly them to Saudi Arabia for Desert Shield and Desert Storm. I took a course in hazard materials shipment and became the person to sign for the equipment. We used government ordering procedures and an accounting number for payment. We then scheduled the airplanes into various civilian and military airports in the U.S., arranged for refueling enroute, and alerted our technicians in-country when the airplanes would arrive. When Desert Storm began, we had to have special transponder codes for our cargo aircraft when they transited Egypt and entered Saudi Arabia. Earlier I mentioned that one of my Air War College classmates had been promoted and was the Deputy Commander of Operations for the Military Airlift Command. I called him, explained our situation and necessity for transponder codes. The next day he called me back that the codes would be coming, they did. Those codes allowed us to transit worldwide with the USAF able to track our civilian cargo airplanes ensuring that they were friendly and authorized into the war zones.

In early 1991 we learned that we were on the short list of contractors for the State Department contract. We received a long list of questions asking about specific operations, personnel, pricing, and schedule. We brought the team together and submitted our answers and new pricing. By this time, I was well into the plan and leading the effort to provide answers. When completed with the proper number of pages and notebooks, our proposal filled a pickup truck. We retained one extra copy should the original get lost in the mail. The proposal was submitted. Now we had to wait for it to be evaluated by the State Department.

A couple of months later we were notified that a team of four people from the State Department would come to our offices for a special briefing and oral negotiations. I was selected to head the team. The night before they were to arrive, our corporate CEO came to hear our presentation and make his inputs. He made several comments and a couple of corrections which I incorporated into the presentation I gave to the State committee the next day. They seemed pleased but came back the second day for oral discussions which I also chaired. At the end of that day, I felt confident that we would win. As they were leaving, I said, "Put us in Coach, we are ready to play." They smiled. That phrase would be used throughout our final negotiations and we won. Later I was told that the CEO initially was upset with me for not taking notes on his recommendations and for being less formal with my comment that we were ready to play. However, a year later he told me that he was most impressed that I took all his recommendations into the briefing, led the oral negotiations, and used that coach analogy to get in the game and win the contract.

Another Move: DynCorp at Patrick AFB, FL (1991-993)

Upon announcement that we had won the contract, DynCorp asked me to be the General Manager and move to Florida. Fortunately, our military move based on our retirement was still available. We packed up our rental house in Austin and prepared to move to Florida. Doug was graduating from Anderson. I went ahead with a dozen DynCorp people to set up the transition office.

I rented an office in Cocoa Beach, FL and our contract gave us 60-days to assume the full contractual responsibilities from the incumbent company. However, after about a week, State asked me to cut it to 30 days because the incumbent was damaging aircraft and parts and they were concerned that there might be sabotage caused by those losing their jobs. Of course, we agreed and doubled down on getting everything under control.

One of the first tasks was to hire the people needed to execute the contract. Because of the poor performance of the previous contractor, we decided to not offer jobs to any of the previous leadership. However, we knew that there were talented, experienced technicians both in the U.S. and at the forward operating locations in South America that would be needed.

I staffed the transition team with experts I had known both in the Air Force and my year at DynCorp. The first call I made was to Gene Davis, the man I had persuaded to not retire but to come to Panama as

Commandant of the Latin American Air Forces Academy. He had moved the Academy to Miami and quickly agreed to retire from the Air Force and come to Patrick. I next added a skilled maintenance officer from my A-10 days. I selected one of my proposal team managers and a highly qualified contract administrator to head our contracts and human resource functions. I needed helicopter experience and added a member of our proposal team who had been an Army helicopter pilot and commander. Our team was set. I then sent Gene to visit the operating locations in Belize, Guatemala, Bolivia and Peru to interview the people that were there. He hired most of them. Many had been with the CIA, contractors, and other agencies in similar conditions including Vietnam. At one stop, Gene was interviewing people in his hotel room. One maintenance technician came in, slammed a handgun on the table, and said, "Let's talk." Gene was not intimidated and did hire him based on his qualifications. Many of the pilots and ground crews had formally worked for oil companies, non-government agencies and the CIA. They knew the environment and were extremely well qualified in their subject areas. As this gentleman demonstrated, they "had been there, done that" and were confident that they could continue.

Our first day taking the contract was very eye opening. We arrived at the hangar on Patrick AFB to find boxes of equipment and components laying on the hangar floor. There were no tags on any of the equipment. Hydraulic and engine oil were oozing onto electrical equipment and airplane avionics. It was a mess.

I brought all the employees together on the hangar floor. We chatted for a couple of minutes then we joined hands and prayed for Divine wisdom and God's direction as we began this formidable task. I asked each of them to go back to their work areas and assess the operation, identifying both strengths and shortcomings. They were to report to the senior staff. I asked the heads of departments to come to my office at 4:00pm to make a preliminary report. At that meeting, each of them reported what they found and made initial recommendations about how to proceed. The meeting lasted until about 8:00pm, but we had a plan in place. I again was reminded of Jeremiah 29:11 that had been our guiding verse in addressing USAF retirement. God does have a plan for us, and it is for good and not for evil. We had committed our ways to Him on retirement and we had done that our first day on this contract.

As we assumed responsibilities for the contract in Florida, a major push against the growing fields was launched in three different countries. It was very successful, and we were off to a good start.

However, not everything was going smoothly. The Department of State could not give us a reliable inventory of the items they were transferring to us. They did have an unaudited inventory from a couple of years back and wanted me to sign for it. I declined because we had identified many items that were on their inventory but not transferred to us. They insisted, and I still refused based on the reality that if I signed the list, it would become the baseline for all future inventories. I would not sign a document that I (and they) knew was wrong.

As an example of the poor records and malfeasance of the previous contractor, the Miami Police found a small jet engine on a highway. It did belong to State and we had it shipped to us for repair. State and we agreed that the inventory would be accepted without signature and without it being binding in future audits. As we accounted for the items transferred and acquired new items, we developed an automated system that clearly delineated exactly what was on hand and where it was stored or installed. We then provided them with both paper and electronic copies of the actual inventory.

Because of the high visibility nature of the contract, I was required to quarterly brief the Department of State on our performance against a specific set of criteria. Our incentive award was based on our performance and on the assessment by State's leadership and contract administrators. The briefing was a major factor in the award. We worked hard to meet contractual requirements and we worked hard to make the presentation clear and positive. We used overhead slides and videos and my presentation usually lasted an hour with questions for another hour. During my two years heading the contract, we were awarded incentives that exceeded other of DynCorp's contracts.

I went to our forward operating bases and flew missions with our team. This picture was taken in Bolivia.

In addition, we received visits from the DynCorp corporate staff. One visit included the Board of Directors. We hosted them by scheduling the hotel and conference rooms, visits and briefings to the operation at Patrick and a dinner cruise on the Indian River followed by dinner at the Melbourne Yacht Club. They were very impressed, and the CEO called to compliment our team on our contract performance and the visit.

While most aspects of the contract were going well above expectations, there were two accidents that were of great concern. One of our aircraft had to make an emergency landing in the jungle. Without consultation with us at DynCorp nor with State Department officials in-country, a decision was made to launch a helicopter with illumination flares to protect the downed aircraft. Unfortunately, the cover helicopter crashed killing the three crewmembers on board. I believe that it was shot down by drug cartel people. But the accident board found that the most probable cause was improperly operating the illuminating flares with one detonating inside the aircraft. About a year later, another night helicopter training mission crash killed one crewmember and seriously injured another. As in the first accident, that flight should not have been flown by that crew, that night. Again, they did not seek approval for the flight but made a spot decision that the training was necessary that night. These accidents point that the failure of local leaders to use good judgment cannot be overcome by senior leaders if those leaders are not fully apprised of the situation before the event is executed. As a three-star general often said, "Don't blame me for the crash if you don't invite me to the pre-flight briefing." I had not been invited to the pre-flight briefing for either one of those crashes.

Living in Florida was both a joy and a challenge. We were pleased with the job and we bought a house two doors from Gene and Judy Davis, the dear friends from Panama who agreed to come to DynCorp with us. Doug moved with us and enrolled in the local college. We joined Melbourne Baptist Church and became active there. The biggest joy was B.J.'s dad moving from Colorado Springs into our home. Her mother had died while we were in Panama and her dad had visited with us there. He couldn't fully care for himself in Colorado, but he was easy to live with in Florida. He loved the beach and the backyard pool. He paid for a heater to be added to the pool, so he could use it on colder days.

At the end of two years, DynCorp decided to move me from Patrick back to the division headquarters in Fort Worth. The Division Manager was a retired AF general whom I had gotten to know, and he wanted me to take over the operations department, but another long-time DynCorp employee was in that position. As a holding position, they made me the head of engineering. While I had an engineering degree, I had never worked as an engineer.

B.J. and her Dad in our Florida home

B.J.'s dad wasn't thrilled to learn we were moving to Texas. Doug decided he had enough of Florida and moved to Austin when we moved to Fort Worth. We rented an apartment, purchased a lot, and began designing our house. The corporate CEO came to visit Fort Worth and the division manager hosted a dinner for the senior staff at his house. When we arrived, the CEO was at the front door and I introduced myself and B.J. He said he knew who we were and wanted to talk to me. He led me to the back yard and around to the back of the pool. We took seats and he said he had a new job for me, but it was in the

Northern Virginia corporate headquarters as President, DynAir Fueling. He explained that the previous president had died of cancer and they were struggling without a leader. I protested a little but agreed to go back for an interview with the president of the parent DynAir company. The interview was a formality since the corporate CEO wanted me. They explained that the company was struggling with its current fueling contracts for the airlines at major airports across the country. My task would be to make the company profitable by winning more business and getting it prepared for sale. I called B.J. and we decided to take the job, moving to Northern Virginia again.

We weren't excited to leave Texas. Derek and Kelly were doing well with both working in their church's Christian school. Doug stayed in Austin, working and going to school. He also served as a campaign manager for a friend who was running for the Texas State Legislature. His time in the Air Force and in Washington had struck a political nerve. He has continued to be very politically astute and has been selected on several national safety committees.

President, DynAir Fueling, Reston, VA (1993-1995)

DynAir agreed to buy out our commitment to build a house in Fort Worth and B.J. and I were free to buy a house in the Reston area. Having lived in Northern Virginia before, B.J. knew that the commuting times could be terrible and insisted on us living near the office. We began our search by driving through neighborhoods that were within a few miles of the office. In one, we saw a beautiful white brick colonial nestled in the trees and called the realtor on the sign. After viewing the house and learning it was a repossession, we began negotiations with the bank, ultimately agreeing to buy the house. We started renovating portions of it the same day we closed. The house was only 15 minutes from the office, even in rush hour. We quickly learned that our dear friends from several previous assignments, Charles and Sindy Schwab, lived across the green belt. It was an additional blessing to be with them again. B.J.'s dad was living with us but couldn't negotiate the stairs. We developed an apartment in our walk-out basement with living room, bedroom and bath that was just perfect for him. We added a stair climber so that he could move between his apartment in the basement to the main floor.

It was an inauspicious beginning at DynAir. I reported to my boss and he walked me down the hall to show me my office. He then left and told me to introduce myself to the others in the company. He was certainly lacking in protocol skills. None the less, I dropped my stuff in the office and went to each office and introduced myself, asked about their responsibilities and learned more about the company. I was soon to learn that others who reported to him would have liked to have the job, especially at my starting salary. Clearly, they were not inclined to give the new guy much help.

As I reviewed the business, it was clear that the airlines had the upper hand in any contract negotiation. There were several other companies as qualified as DynAir to operate airport fuel farms and facilities and put fuel in the airplanes. In addition, they knew the pricing structure at every airport. We were in a serious disadvantage in trying to raise prices or to even win additional contracts at other airports. My first task was to call the fueling departments at each of our customer airlines and at each airport. I then began to personally visit each of them. I could learn where we were strong and where we needed help. Each customer was willing to give a candid evaluation if they felt I would take their recommendations. I did. Soon we were improving our performance and gaining small fee increases.

I wanted to expand into general aviation airports that serviced corporate jet traffic. Profit margin on fuel for corporate jets was a much higher percentage than that for the airlines, primarily because the corporate jets could not take as much fuel. To go into a new small airport, we had to either build or assume the costs of a fuel storage facility, trucks, personnel, and offices. It could have been profitable at airports such as Reno where we had an airline operation. However,

DynCorp corporate board of directors had decided they wanted to sell DynAir to concentrate on government services business.

We enjoyed being in Northern Virginia and our CEO began moving both B.J. and me into more prominent roles. We often represented him and DynCorp at diplomatic functions and corporate gatherings. He was invited to accompany a government sponsored business trip to Europe, and he asked me to make the arrangements. At the last minute, he had to cancel. I asked him if he would like me to go. He said not to go, but he appreciated the offer. Tragically, the airplane crashed attempting a low visibility approach into a mountainous airport. All aboard died. Both he and I were sorry for those who did go on the trip and very happy that we did not. Once again, God was watching over us and arranged that we would not be on that trip.

As usual, we quickly found a great church and B.J. began singing with the excellent choir. We enjoyed being near Charles and Sindy and other friends in the area. We were able to enjoy our time share at Bryce Mountain that we had purchased during our earlier assignment at the Pentagon.

I called three of my Academy Classmates and invited them to dinner at a local restaurant. I picked them because of their friendship, but primarily because of their success in disparate activities. One was a retired AF brigadier general, another a serial entrepreneur, and the third an astronaut that would later become the acting director of NASA. We knew each other as classmates at The Academy and we had each been successful in the Air Force and in civilian activities after retirement. We talked about how we could be both friendly advisors to each other and accountability partners. We continued to meet at least once a quarter for as long as I was in Northern Virginia. I valued their wise advice and counsel and I think they valued mine. I strongly recommend fostering those kinds of relationships where confidentiality is respected and mutual time valued.

We loved living in Northern Virginia and enjoyed the big colonial house. Its curbside appeal was more impressive than its true value.

We had worked hard on the landscaping and trees as well as the inside. At Christmas we decorated the bushes with lights and the house with festive colors and a beautiful tree. We hosted a DynCorp/DynAir party the first Christmas. My boss loved the house but said he was paying us too much if we could afford it. Interestingly, he was in the process of building a new house that he would pay several times more than we had paid for this one.

B.J.'s dad was enjoying his basement apartment and he was negotiating the stair climber with his walker and travel between floors as he wished. All worked well until we took him on a road trip to enjoy the Fall colors in the mountains. We stopped for breakfast. As we were walking out, I was beside him and B.J. behind him. A rock stopped a wheel on the walker, and he fell hard to the ground and was in pain. We loaded him in our car, returned to the hospital in Reston, and learned he had shattered his hip. He was never able to walk again. We found a nice nursing home and B.J. visited him nearly every day. His injury was our great disappointment of his time with us. We often ask ourselves what we could have done to prevent it; but we had tried by walking close to him. Our mistake was assuming he was more mobile than he really was.

Doug Watson Comes to Washington with a Friend

Doug called us about coming to Virginia for Christmas. Of course, we agreed. He then asked if he could bring a friend. I asked if this friend was of the female type. He said yes but explained that they were just good friends from the same Sunday School class, and he would like to show her Washington. We got her mother's phone number and B.J. called to explain how the visit would work. We used miles to fly them from Austin to Dulles Airport and met them at the airport. She was a lovely lady and we enjoyed meeting her.

The following Spring Break, Doug called again. Christy would come with him for the holiday. True to his word, Doug took her on the Metro to the Washington tourist sites and they had a great time. We could see that the romance was blossoming. It was clear that they had a longer-term relationship in mind, and we were happy. Soon we were told we would be moving back to Texas. We were especially happy that we would be closer to them.

Mr. and Mrs. Doug Watson

Moving back to Fort Worth (1995-1996)

Our efforts at DynAir Fueling did improve our bottom line and consistent cash flow. In addition, the larger DynAir company improved its balance sheet. As the two businesses improved, they became a more attractive acquisition. At my two-year point, DynAir and DynAir Fueling were purchased by a European firm. I was offered the opportunity to stay as president of the new DynAir Fueling company and would have reported to the European headquarters. I wasn't excited to transfer to the new company. I would have preferred to stay in Virginia with DynCorp, but there were no positions available.

However, the president of the DynCorp Aviation Services company in Fort Worth made a strong pitch for me to come back to work for him. He was the same person that had moved me from Florida to the short time at Fort Worth. Again, his plan was for me to become the VP of Operations.

After talking to the DynCorp CEO and senior staff and consultation with B.J., we decided to accept the offer to return to Texas. While there was the expectation that I would become the head of operations, the incumbent was still the same guy that had hired me about five years earlier and he wouldn't retire. Consequently, I was shoved into being the Director of Marketing with the plan that I would quickly move to head operations. While I had been successful in developing proposals and winning business in my previous DynCorp positions, marketing wasn't my best fit. However, I did have a strong background and interest in Operations. I was looking forward to moving to head the Operations Division.

We moved to Fort Worth and purchased a nice home in Weatherford, about 25 miles west of Fort Worth. I began assuming the marketing chores and was having success. On a trip to DynCorp headquarters, my boss made a presentation that didn't go well, and he immediately resigned. I was left in the cold with a job in which I wasn't especially qualified, the boss that recruited me leaving under a cloud, and the director of operations unhappy that I was there.

DynCorp started a search for a new president of the Fort Worth aviation services company. I submitted my name. However, it was clear that they wanted to go toward a technology guru to attack more profitable technology services. He was hired from the outside. Soon it became obvious that he wanted to replace me with a technology marketing guy, and I was offered a separation package and outplacement assistance. For the first time since I was old enough to push a lawn mower, I was out of work and income. However, now I had a wife and a big house with a big mortgage to support.

Chapter 17: Entering the Job Search Morass (1996-2018)

DynCorp initially offered me one week of severance for each year of my employment which resulted in only 5 weeks of continued pay and benefits. I was also offered six months of job search assistance. I did not feel that the offer was appropriate for my situation and wrote a letter to the CEO outlining some of the successes of my career at DynCorp, reminding him that he had recommended that I turn down the continuance at DynAir Fueling and accept the Fort Worth position, and that he had persuaded me to leave Fort Worth to go to DynAir Fueling two years before. He bought the argument and increased the severance to six months.

I had never searched for a job. Instead, I was offered ever increasing job opportunities in both the Air Force and DynCorp. Fortunately, I learned many lessons of job hunting during my time at the out-placement agency. Of course, lessons started with writing a resume, then a cover letter, and interviewing techniques. Those lessons have led to me helping many, many others find jobs over the years since I had to find my first one.

The job search was painful. I sent scores of resumes and had several interviews. At a NBAA Conference, I was introduced to Trajen Flight Services, a small company headquartered in Bryan, Texas. I accepted the offer to be the general manager of their new facility at the former Mather Air Force Base in Sacramento, California. Again, I would be separated from B.J. and living in a corporate apartment. I would fly from Fort Worth to Sacramento early on Monday and return Friday evening, usually on the redeye. In addition to operating the refueling systems and transient aircraft support, Trajen had a contract to operate two Beechcraft 1900 commuter aircraft owned by major software company. We shuttled its company personnel with two flights in the morning, one at noon, and two in the evening to/from San Jose, CA. They were transported between their offices and the airfield in specially configured and comfortable buses which permitted them to continue to work on their laptops while enroute. They also could work on the laptops while airborne. After a month or so, I convinced everyone that I should checkout as a co-pilot in the airplanes and flew once or twice a week on the shuttle missions.

Even though I was enjoying the job and the people, I kept circulating my resume. After about six months I received a call that Trinity Industries in Fort Worth would like to talk with me, and we arranged an interview while the VP was skiing in California. They made me an offer I couldn't refuse; I would be back in Fort Worth with B.J. and the income would cover our financial responsibilities.

Before leaving Trajen, I met with the owner. I knew he wanted to sell the company and I arranged meetings for him with an acquisition/merger company. As the negotiations progressed, I drafted an agreement that he would pay me a commission based on the sales price and he signed it. I worked many, many hours in developing spread sheets, negotiating points and evaluating the company. Unknown to me, he was using my data to work a side deal with another company that I had told him about. He sold the company to the side deal company and refused to pay me a commission. In fact, he didn't tell me about the sale until after I called him about a rumor I had heard. The moral of the story is that you must have every little detail in legalese writing. I could have sued him. But after consulting with B.J. we decided that we were not led to do that. Had he sold to the company that I brought him, my commission would have been well over a half million dollars.

Back in Fort Worth (1996-2000)

Trinity Industries is a large rail car and equipment company. One of its plants in Fort Worth produced rail car parts, baggage handling systems for airports, and passenger boarding bridges that connect the air terminal to the airplane.

My direction was to be the General Manager of the Stearns Airport Systems portion and Trinity would continue to operate the rail car portion of the plant. It became clear very early that Trinity wanted to divest the Stearns airport equipment portion and I began developing a plan to sell it.

On a trip to an airport conference/exposition in Europe, I arranged a meeting with Thyssen, one of our boarding bridge competitors. I explained our desire to sell the assets of the company and they were very interested but didn't want to buy the baggage handling manufacturing portion of the business. I then contacted a person that was installing our baggage systems and asked him if he would like to buy it.

Over the next several months, I developed the plan to sell the boarding bridge business to Thyssen and the baggage systems to the other company. We continued to service our current customers and win new ones to increase the value of the companies. Ultimately the plan was consummated, and I became the president of the new Thyssen-Stearns Airport Services Company.

Thyssen-Stearns Airport Systems (2000-2002)

We could not stay in the Trinity factory. We had to find another facility. After an extensive search in the Fort Worth area, we moved into a large former manufacturing company. However, it had not been used in many years and required hours of clean up, move of machines from Trinity into the acquired facility, and hire of personnel. B.J. and I spent the first weekend cleaning the offices of dirt, insects, and disuse. We brought in our own wireless telephones until the phone company could install multiple lines. Amazingly, we were in full operation in less than 30 days. B.J. came on board as an unpaid receptionist until we could hire a full time, paid replacement.

The transition was not smooth. Our negotiations were with the German division of Thyssen and went well. However, they decided to consolidate the boarding bridge business under their Spanish operation giving them plants in Germany, Spain, and ours in the U.S. My counterpart German manager left Thyssen. His Spanish replacement was not as capable. Moreover, they sent plant managers from both Germany and Spain to "standardize" operations. Unfortunately, the European operations were not standardized and there was significant disagreement between them about how to set up the U.S. factory. The good news was that Thyssen had assigned a young MBA as the CFO who reported both to me and to Germany. Alex Pfurr became the intermediary to smooth out the kinks in the transition. He was very bright and clearly understood the Thyssen way of business. Based on his abilities, I also made him the Director of Marketing and our sales numbers dramatically improved.

After two years, the Spanish leadership wanted to send one of their people to the U.S. to learn more about U.S. operations and sales and asked me to resign. I agreed to leave after I completed a large project to manufacture and install the boarding bridges at the new international terminal, Terminal D, at Dallas Fort Worth (DFW) airport. and left the company. I was given a severance package and was happy to move on.

Alex Pfurr quickly moved up in the company. Soon after I left, he moved to Spain to head that operation. After a couple of years, he moved back to Germany into corporate leadership. He was the driving force behind Thyssen Airport Systems becoming a global company with manufacturing in Germany, Spain, U.S., and China. They were very kind to invite B.J. and me to the celebration of building the 1000th boarding bridge in the facility that we had started. We were honored to be included and recognized by the company and the people that had made the success.

We became close friends with Alex and his family. B.J. and I attended his wedding in Germany and promised his and Mieke's families that we would take great care of them. We did. And, we have been to Germany to visit them. In 2017 their older daughter, Isabella, came with Alex on his business trip. We gave her tours of horse farms and airplane facilities and took her on our son Doug's boat to enjoy the lake. In 2018, the entire family: Alex, Meike, Isabella and the younger daughter, Beatrice, toured the U.S. Again, we hosted them here, including another trip to the lake, Mexican food, the Fort Worth Stockyards, and other very Texas things to do.

BJAerospace LLC (2002-Present)

Using the time and severance from Thyssen, we started BJAerospace LLC, a consulting company that has become the foundation for several entrepreneurial activities. It is named after B.J. who is the majority owner and chair. The company has worked with both large and small corporations in pilot training, aircraft modification, aircraft acquisition and sales, corporate mergers, and contract pilot services.

Initially, an Academy classmate, co-worker in Panama, and very good friend called asking if I was interested in helping him write a training program for the midlife update on the F-16. The answer was a quick, "Yes." I worked for him at Lockheed Martin about six months preparing the program. We both went to The Netherlands to present the program to European instructor pilots who would take the course we developed and in-flight instruction to the squadron pilots.

As we finished this program, I applied for a full-time job at Lockheed Martin in the same division I had been working. I was hired and would be responsible for managing development of ground equipment. While very appreciative of having the job and income, I quickly became bored and frustrated with trying to push my projects through the Lockheed Martin bureaucracy. I called a friend from our days at the Pentagon and reconnection through Bible Study Fellowship. He had left Lockheed Martin for a small company modifying airplanes for the Air Force. It sounded exciting and he invited me to visit and learn more.

He showed me around the company and introduced me to the president who asked for my resume. Several visits later they offered me a job as a program manager which I quickly accepted. Unfortunately, during the period between being offered the job and signing on board, I was diagnosed with prostate cancer. After biopsies and consultation with several doctors, it was obvious that the cancer was aggressive and needed to be quickly removed. I called the president explaining my situation and offering him two alternatives: 1) He could withdraw the offer or 2) I would continue to come on board with the understanding that surgery would take me out of the office for a week. Fortunately, he chose the second option not knowing if the surgery would be effective or if I would be able to return. I had the surgery by the newly approved Da Vinci robot assisted surgery, and it was successful. After a week, I was in my new job.

The cancer was a scare. However, with God's blessing and the surgery, I have been cancer-free for fifteen years.

I immediately became involved in modifying Swiss-built Pilatus airplanes with reconnaissance equipment. In addition, I was the Program Manager for building a new hangar. A few weeks after I joined them, the company was purchased by a large government contractor. We quickly went from an entrepreneurial, fast acting company to one saddled by paper work and leadership who knew nothing about aircraft or modifying them.

Regardless, I enjoyed four years of modifying airplanes with my friend. We made major strides in adapting civilian aircraft for military purposes. In addition to the Pilatus, we installed Hellfire missiles on Cessna Caravans, made major modifications to C-130s, installed surveillance systems on Citation Jets and Piper aircraft, and serviced these systems for the military and Customs and Border Protection. When it became time to retire, both my friend and I retired the same day. The company went through a serious downturn after we left but has been resurrected by a very talented man whom we had the privilege of mentoring.

After leaving ATK, a friend whose airplane I had been flying as a contract pilot called asking me to come to his company to straighten out the administrative procedures of his large roofing company. When I arrived, there were no systems to track what projects were upcoming and could be bid, which bids had been submitted, the status of bids, or following schedules and budgets. In a couple of months, I designed and implemented simple Excel spreadsheets, updated, and posted for all project managers and corporate leadership to observe and manage. A weekly staff meeting was initiated to discuss what has happened and what was projected to happen. The company and teamwork improved. I continued to manage and fly his airplane. In about a year, things were running smoothly and there was a need to sell the airplane. Having completed my agreed tasks, I asked to leave the company and try real retirement.

Dr. Ken Reed and I met in 1992 when I offered our T-34 for sale and he asked to lease it. He chose not to execute the purchase and we sold it to someone else. When we came back to DFW in 1995 I called him. He explained he wanted to buy another T-34 and we worked together to find the right airplane. He bought that airplane and allowed me to fly it as I wished for the next 22 years.

Dr. Reed also bought a Fouga Magister aircraft that is a French-built jet trainer. It was followed by an L-39 Czechoslovakian-built jet trainer. He was kind to include me in his checkouts and on his insurance. We flew in several airshows and earned our FAA certification for formations and for unrestricted airspeed and low altitude fly-bys.

Scott Tankersley is another pilot friend whom I met in Sunday School. He has owned several airplanes and has included me as an instructor and second pilot in each. Again, he included me in the checkouts and insurances which permits me to fly with him or as pilot in command should he not be available.

BJAerospace continues to be the umbrella company through which we conduct pilot training, pilot services, business and aviation consulting, and aircraft sales/purchase. I am blessed to be called to fly corporately owned twin-engine Cessna Aircraft and I am a back up pilot on Cessna Citation jets. It is unfortunate that we do not have an airplane suitable to teach our grandchildren the joys of flight, they do fly with me when the opening is presented.

The FAA recently presented me with the Wright Brothers Master Pilot Award which recognizes more than 50 years flying as pilot-in-command with no accidents or FAA violations.

My flying goal is to continue to fly for as long as the opportunities are presented, and I am healthy. One of my new goals is to be paid to be a pilot when I am 80 years old.

Chapter 18: Looking Beyond the Horizon

Meanwhile, Back Home in Indiana

While I was eager to leave Indiana to go to the Air Force Academy in 1960, I was always ready to return there to visit family. Mom and Dad were in good health and continued to operate the store and farm for many more years. Our entire family always looked forward to visiting and doing all the things that can only be done on a farm. The boys loved driving the lawn mower, then the same tractor that I had driven.

Grandpa Watson had a fishing boat and we took every opportunity to take it to local ponds and Sullivan Lake for fishing. On one excursion on Uncle Gay's pond, Doug hooked a big fish and we got him to the edge of the boat before he gave us one look, broke the line, and headed toward the bottom. As the grandparents aged, Dad came up with one rule for our boys: Only one activity per day. They could fish or go to the farm, but not on the same day.

When Brother Bill returned from Vietnam, he attended Vincennes University and received an FAA pilot license for airplanes and instruments. More importantly, he met and married Glenda in 1990. They moved to nearby Sullivan and Bill took a job driving a caterpillar at a coal-fired power station. However, they had higher goals. They began with a backhoe and worked weekends to accumulate enough resources to quit the power plant job, purchase larger excavating equipment, and start their own business. They have been very successful in expanding their business, purchasing additional farm land, and raising two daughters, Susan and Sallie.

Bill and Glenda
Susan, Rob, Nick and Will
Sallie and Andrew

When Dad was retiring, he asked Bill and me to split the farm. The three of us decided on the manner to split the acreage and Dad had the papers developed. After several years B.J. and I decided we would not move back to Indiana. Bill offered to purchase our part of the farm. He could do a much better job in managing it and it would put the original property back together. He was very kind to pay us the market price. And, he is kind to drive us through the woods in his jeep showing us the improvements he has made.

Bill continued flying by purchasing an aircraft. A heart attack prompted him to sell the first aircraft. Fortunately, his heart has recovered, and he has owned two aircraft since then. He built a sod runway on his farm and keeps and flies his airplane from his back yard. While we don't get together often enough, we have enjoyed a cruise to Alaska and a beach vacation with Bill and Glenda and in exchanging visits with them. They and the rest of their family are very special to all of us Texas Watsons.

Dad and Mom in Bill's yard
Perhaps the last picture of them together

We could never repay Bill and Glenda for the selfless efforts they expended to care for Mom and Dad over many years. They handled the administrative and financial affairs, often visited them, directed the sale of property and even arranged for their funerals. Later they did a similar job for Aunt Jeanette.

Watson Family Updated to 2019

B.J and I moved into an "Active Adult Community" in 2007. We love living at Robson Ranch, Denton, Texas, 30 miles north of Fort Worth.

There are several clubs. B.J. is active and has served on the Boards of the Music Club and Women's Club. She especially enjoys singing with the Robson Singers and has been a featured soloist in a couple of their concerts. We have wonderful friends with whom we have travelled locally and internationally and enjoy just getting together.

We continue to be very active in our church, Denton Bible Church, and are preparing to be leaders in their marriage ministries.

Derek and Kelly live in Tyler, about 150 miles east of us. Brooke was born in 1999 and is studying to be a physical therapist assistant. As previously mentioned, we like to refer to her as our Favorite Granddaughter and she is prompt to remind us that she is our only granddaughter. She has recently become engaged with the wedding set for May 2019. Derek owns a business development company primarily working for his A&M roommate, Brian Jacobe. He is instrumental in marketing and securing construction contracts. Kelly has been a fantastic care giver for her grandmother and mother. The entire family is very active in their church with Derek first serving as Headmaster of their school for 11 years and is now serving as an associate pastor. Kelly plays the piano, and Brooke is in the orchestra and choir. They have travelled extensively to Haiti and Kenya to minister with sister churches there.

Doug and Christy were married in her church in her home town of Corpus Christi, and began their life together in Austin. Doug moved rapidly from construction management into construction safety; first for a contractor in Austin, then the Austin General Contractors' Association. He was recruited to a similar position in Houston, then to Dallas. We were excited when they moved to Denton only twenty minutes from our house. They added Garrett and Carter in Austin and Wesley in Houston. Christy gave up her career with IBM when Garrett joined the family. However, she is more than busy with three very active boys and volunteers in their schools. All three boys are doing much better in school than did I. Doug is the Regional Director of Safety for a very large construction firm and is responsible for huge projects across Texas, Louisiana, Arkansas, Oklahoma and New Mexico.

We often get the family together. Christmas 2018 was an opportunity to capture the entire family in one picture.

The Watson Family Christmas 2018
Mom and Dad in Front.
Christy and Doug are behind me with their three boys, Garrett (16), Carter (13), and Wesley (11).
Behind Mom is Kelly, Derek and Brooke, and Brooke's fiancé Stephen.

We have been abundantly blessed for more than the past half century and we are continuing to be blessed with a wonderful family, great friends, and an active lifestyle. While we are unable to see beyond the horizon, we have great faith that the future will be as exciting and fulfilling as the past has been.

**We know not what lies beyond our horizon.
But we know who holds our future**

Chapter 19: Life Lessons Learned Along the Way

While most of the following has been addressed earlier in this book, I wanted to summarize the important lessons that B.J. and I have learned along the way. Perhaps some readers will want to cut to this section. If they glean a few nuggets here, my efforts will have been successful.

1.) Christ is the Center

We are not a "religious" family, but we have a relationship with Jesus. But it was clear from my early life that Christ was the center of the Watson family. Mom and Dad led us to Sunday School and Church. Through that leadership, I accepted Jesus Christ as my Savior and Lord when I was in Junior High School. As I grew older and moved away from the little church on the corner, I drifted away from a close relationship with Jesus. Nonetheless, Jesus was always on my mind and I attended Bible Studies and Chapel at The Academy.

When B.J. and I became more serious in our dating relationship, we had a frank discussion and concluded that together we would find a church in which we could commit our lives and service to Christ. We knelt at our honeymoon bedside, prayed and dedicated our marriage to the Lord on our first night. In every subsequent move we established the highest priority to find a Bible-Centered church. And we committed to raising our family with Christ as the center.

The phrase, "What Would Jesus Do?" is not empty in the Watson family. While we often fail and must seek His forgiveness, we daily strive to live as Christ would have us live.

Our boys have brought this core value into their own homes and families. Derek and Kelly serve in the church where they met, and Brooke is active there as well. Doug and Christy met in Sunday School in Austin. They were married in her home church and they have a

Christ-centered home. Their boys have each accepted Christ as Savior and Lord and are walking with him.

B.J. and I are most proud of the Christian legacy that began when we were dating, was consummated on our wedding night, and has consistently improved as we have committed, studied, and served Him.

2.) Regardless of the Circumstances, Hard Work Is Rewarded

Mom and Dad had started college. However, The Depression sapped family resources and they had to drop out to work to add to their respective family's incomes. They found ways to overcome and see a future together. From the fields of Indiana and Arkansas to the steel mills of Indiana, they moved for greater opportunity to achieve their dream. They were quick to save their money and establish economic viability to avoid the disaster experienced in the Great Depression. They also developed a regular spending habit that allowed disciplined savings. One of Dad's favorite sayings on the subject was, "It doesn't matter how much money you make, it matters how much you save." The emphasis on "save" was to clearly establish his point.

I started mowing lawns, working in our store, and driving tractors for neighbor farmers at an early age. In my senior year of high school and the following summers I worked as an apprentice electrician. Dad established a bank account for me, and we would deposit my earnings on a regular basis. He tried to ingrain a savings mind set. That emphasis stayed with me throughout the Air Force and civilian careers and has been passed on to our boys.

We were rewarded with rapid promotions in both military and civilian jobs. The accelerated advancement meant more income and increased responsibilities, both of which we appreciated. Yet, the down side of longer hours, more travel, and increased time away from family was a cost that had to be shouldered. After all has been considered, I would do it again with a little more discretion in which jobs I took and which ones I rejected.

3.) Set Goals, Believe in Them, Keep Focused on Them, Work Toward Them

I had an early goal of attending and graduating from the Air Force Academy. When we lived in Hammond, my parents used to drive by Midway Airport, and we would watch the airplanes. Later in Graysville, Uncle Gay told me about some of his WWII flying experiences. I believe that God placed the desire to a pilot in my heart at the moment of my conception. Over the years it has become more apparent that God does have a plan for us (Jeremiah 29:11). However, we need to spend time with Him to determine His plan.

The seed began to germinate and grow, and I applied for entrance into the Academy Class of 1962. I was not accepted that year or even the next. I applied the third time for the Class of 1964 and was an alternate. But I kept believing and was ultimately accepted when a primary candidate declined the appointment. It was providential that I was not accepted the first two times. I wasn't prepared and could not have graduated. The Class of 1964 was and is a fantastic class of super achievers and I am blessed to have graduated with them.

In pilot training I set the goal of being near the top of the class and worked hard in academics, flying, and sports to achieve the goal. B.J. was my greatest supporter and her efforts significantly contributed to my being a Distinguished Graduate. Together we achieved the goal and we got our first choice of airplanes and bases.

Over the following half century, we prayerfully sought the Lord, listened for His direction, and committed our plans to follow Him. We often had setbacks, but we stayed focused on the goals and invested our time and energizes toward those goals and His plans. He closed some doors and He opened other doors. We like the Amplified Version of Proverbs 16:3, *"Commit your works to the Lord (submit and trust them to Him), and your plans will succeed (if you respond to His will and guidance)."*

One of the saddest songs often sung at a funeral is *"I did it my way."* On the contrary, our goal is to do it God's way. Learn to not only talk to the Lord about your plans, but also to hear from Him through His Word, His people, and the small voice in your mind. If you are having trouble going to sleep, maybe it isn't the pizza before bed. Ask the Lord if He is trying to speak to you.

Our goal is to finish strong by helping others through mentoring, Bible studies, consulting, or training pilots. When asked if I am going to "slow down", I quickly reply "NO!". As long as God gives me health and a very supportive wife, I will strive to the mark of the high calling of Christ. One of my flying goals is to be paid for flying at age 80. Both B.J. and I enjoy passing some of our Life Lessons to our family and in counselling.

4.) Integrity and Honesty Are Core Values and the Foundation of Character

Throughout my lifetime our entire family has lived by "our word is our bond." As I grew and began working for other farmers and buying/selling livestock and grain, I learned that the Watson name was well respected throughout the community. Neither we nor many of our neighbor farmers could afford to own all the equipment necessary to plant, cultivate, and harvest crops. We often borrowed each other's equipment. We also serviced, repaired and cleaned it before we returned it to the owner. Large parcels of property were negotiated with a handshake.

When I arrived at The Academy, there was great emphasis placed on the Honor Code, *"We will not lie, cheat, or steal nor tolerate among us those who do."* Without it being so poignantly articulated, I had lived that way all my life. It was easy to agree to live by the Code both at the Academy and following.

The Golden Rule is founded on integrity and honesty. We know that we have been blessed by God's favor and we are obligated to share that blessing with others. We commit our tithes and offerings to the church where we are members. We have opened our home to girls who needed a place to stay while working or going to school. When we built our current home, we added a casita guest suite. When a close friend's home burned, they stayed in it the first night and were able to get a shower, collect themselves, before finding a rental. A couple who started and are operating a Bible Training Center in Kenya stayed with us a month before going to Kenya and two months after returning while their new home was being built.

5.) Leadership by Example and Influence

Growing up our parents encouraged us to get involved in school, sports, music and other activities and we moved up in leadership positions. I was only average in sports. However, I seemed to excel in 4-H where I became a local and county leader and mentor.
Of course, the Air Force Academy and a career in the active Air Force placed me into leadership and mentoring positions. I have tried to transfer those skills into our children, grandchildren, and church friends. I am not humble in bragging on them. They have become leaders in their families, churches, work, and school and are excelling well beyond my accomplishments.

We are committed to leadership by example. We strive to do more than we ask others to do. We establish high standards for ourselves, our family and our team. Integrity is a core principle of good leadership. Another core principle is to first take care of your teammates, then they will achieve greater results.

We used leadership skills learned along the way throughout our everyday lives. Sometimes the boys and I would stand on a street corner and look up or point to see how many people would voluntarily join us. Or we would start a second line to get into a crowded venue. We are leaders in the churches we attend. Unfortunately, leadership isn't taught in seminaries. Often young seminary graduates become head pastors of churches without the organizational and leadership skills necessary to fully lead the church. We have come alongside them and contributed our talents and experience to help them grow. As would be expected, sometimes they didn't appreciate our recommendations. In every case we have submitted to the pastor or we have quietly left the church without criticizing them.

The Bible is filled with examples of both good and bad leadership. The book of Nehemiah is an excellent study on good leadership. Both Chronicles and Kings candidly discuss the good and bad kings of Israel. First Timothy, Chapter 3, clearly establishes the criteria for selecting leaders for the church. We would all be better by stepping up to those requirements as we desire to be leaders. Jesus was the ultimate leader and was the role model for "servant-leader".

6.) Education

Mom and Dad attended college for as long as their depression-level money allowed. They set education goals for us, required that we studied, and encouraged us to go for ever increasing levels of education.

Partly because of the small school and limited academic program, I struggled throughout college. However, persistence and hard work resulted in a BS in Engineering from the Air Force Academy, an MS in Operations Management from the University of Southern California, and Distinguished Graduate from both Pilot Training and the Air War College.

Clearly, not all education is learned in the halls of academia. Rather, our core value of education is that each person finds their God-given talent and ability, then pursues it with education appropriate to that calling. Often on the job training is more valuable than formal schooling. Education is a life-long enterprise.

B.J. and I are very excited that the boys, their wives and their children have continued to study and take advantage of non-academic education in their travels and daily lives.

7.) The Role of Money: Money is a useful servant, but a terrible master.

I grew up in a very entrepreneurial family. We owned and operated the country store and farm and Dad worked in the factory. Accordingly, we had diversified income and responsibilities. While there was usually a positive cash flow, weather often caused low crop yields and some of our store's customers were late paying their bills. Early we learned to control expenses.

Marriage brings a second set of money values. B.J. and I have worked together to ensure that we have money left at the end of the month. We learned to diversify our incomes by my flying, home based businesses, and by starting BJAerospace LLC. But, as Dad often taught; "It isn't how much money you make, it is how much you <u>keep</u>." We are still working on that lesson.

When we retired from the Air Force, we learned about 401Ks, investing in company stock, and getting professional assistance from a financial advisor. We have built a small nest egg that meets our needs and will help educate our grandchildren.

Here are our five lessons learned about money:
A.) Work hard and diversify sources of income.
B.) Have a spending plan. Don't spend all that you make. Learn to save, even if a little, every pay check.
C.) Pay your tithes first, then yourself in savings, before you buy stuff.
D.) Make wise investments and let the capital and interest grow.
E.) Don't try to keep up with the Joneses.

Never buy something you don't need with money you don't have to impress someone you don't like. And, don't buy on an impulse; think about it.

8.) Important Versus Urgent

Too often we slight what is important to concentrate on the urgent. This concept has been often illustrated by the old saying, "It is difficult to remember that the objective is to drain the swamp when alligators are biting at your rearward parts."

In flying we often refer to this challenge as "target fixation." Some pilots are so fixated on trying to hit the target that they fail to consider other factors such as terrain, wingmen, g-loading, airspeed, and altitude and fly into the target or fail to pull out from a dive. Commercial airliners have run out of fuel or flown into the Everglades while concentrating on a minor issue such as a flashing light and ignoring the criticality of basic flying.

There have been many times in my career that the urgency of work took precedence over what was most important at home. The assignment to the OJCS in the Pentagon was the biggest challenge. The work was demanding of both time and body. The result of expending the body at work was not having the emotional or physical strength needed when I was home. The damage was not as much to me as it was to the family deprived of me. It was certainly a critical time in our nation with the Iranians holding American hostages and I was making significant contributions to our national efforts. The family understood why I needed to be away from home. Nonetheless, they paid a price for my absence. Families are part of us all the time, at work, at home, wherever.

9.) Finish Strong

B.J. has been an exemplary wife and mother and has often been the "dad" as well. I cannot thank her enough for her contributions to our family. Whether I was gone to Vietnam early in our marriage, on a military deployment or operation, or traveling for business in our civilian life, she kept things rolling. The boys did well in school, they made good choices, and they are now outstanding men and dads. She deserves the credit.

Throughout my life there have been people who blessed me with excellent guidance and who kept me on a rather narrow life path. Of course, parents are our first level of influence and mentoring and mine did an excellent job. But bosses, friends, colleagues, pastors and even casual conversations have planted seeds that have yielded successful crops of achievement.

B.J. and I have set our goal to finish strong by replicating some of the wise counsel and advice that we have received. We have enjoyed facilitating and teaching Bible studies, financial management classes, and career development programs. We are embarking to facilitate a formal Re/Engage marriage program for couples in our church.

We are blessed with two other neighborhood couples who sow good seed into our lives and who have our permission to point out any issues or inconsistencies in how we are living. We share with them in Bible Studies, travel and just having a meal. We are also accountable to our pastors.

Our immense joy is in working with our children and grandchildren. Sometimes, we are very direct in providing guidance. But most of the time we make suggestions and tell stories that illustrate what we would like for them to learn on their own. We are prayerful that they will find this autobiography helpful in determining the Watson legacy. We also pray that they will expand upon it and establish a strong legacy for their children and their children's children for those generations that follow. We are honored that all have continued to embrace and complete the core values that we tried to establish. We are very proud of them, not for what we have done, but for what they are doing and for their high standards of character.

Our greatest goal is to live a life of integrity, honesty, and purpose and at the end hear:

"Well done, good and faithful servant. You have been faithful and trustworthy over a few things. … Enter and share in the joy of your Master."

(Matthew 25:21 AMP)

Made in the USA
Columbia, SC
27 March 2019